A Tu

Cookbook

BULGARIA

Black Sea

Edirne•
GREECE

•Istanbul

Sea of
Marmara

•Adapazari

•Bursa

•Ankara

LESBOS

•Manisa

CHIOS   •Izmir   A N A T O L I A   Görem

Aegean   SAMOS   •Ephesus   Neveshi
Sea
                                                    •Konya

                  •Bodrum
                      •Marmaris   •Antalya   TOROS MOUN
                        •Fethiye   Mersin
                        •Olu Deniz   •Alanya

            RHODES

        Mediterranean   CYPRUS
              Sea

A Turkish Cookbook

Arto der Haroutunian

Ebury Press
London

NOTE

All recipes serve 6 people
unless otherwise stated.

The ingredients given in
this book are in both
metric and imperial measures.
Use either one or the other
as they are not interchangeable.

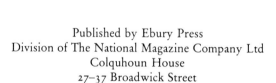

Published by Ebury Press
Division of The National Magazine Company Ltd
Colquhoun House
27–37 Broadwick Street
London WIV IFR

First impression 1987

ISBN 0 85223 630 1 (hardback)
0 85223 615 8 (paperback)

Edited by Yvonne McFarlane and Sue Wason
Designed by Harry Green
Illustrations by Anne Ormerod

Computerset by MFK Typesetting Ltd, Hitchin, Herts
Printed in Great Britain at the University Press, Cambridge

CONTENTS

INTRODUCTION

'I am a Turk; my faith and my race are mighty.'

MEHMET EMIN (POET)

On 21 October, 1923, with a salute of 101 guns which thundered across the skies, the Turkish Republic was born amidst wars, plagues, massacres and fratricide. The Caesarean birth killed the mother – the Ottoman Empire – while the child saw the light of day helpless and kinless. Decades later, Turkey still stands alone, surrounded by historic enemies and unsure of her position in the family of nations.

The name Turkey has been used (by the Europeans) for Turkish-speaking Anatolia almost since its conquest by the Seljuks in the eleventh century, though the history of the country is astoundingly long – almost 10,000 years – and the earliest inhabitants have been traced back to 7500 B.C. Hittites, Phrygians, Lydians, Persians and Romans all swept through the area and established their civilisations here. 'In the imperial society of the Ottomans the ethnic term "Turk" was little used and then chiefly in a rather derogatory sense, to designate the Turkoman nomads or later the ignorant and uncouth Turkish-speaking peasants of the Anatolian villages. To apply it to an Ottoman gentleman of Constantinople would have been an insult'.[1]

The Turks originated in Central Asia, Siberia and the great northern plains on either side of the Ural Mountains. According to legend, Turks came from the mythical land of Turan where they lived in wealth and splendour. A great leader called Feridun divided his lands between his two sons, giving Iran to Ir and Turan to Tur. People who now call themselves Turks were better known to the Chinese as T'u-kin. They came from the eastern frontiers of the Islamic Califate in Central Asia and penetrated the Arab-ruled lands as slaves and mercenaries fighting for Islam. There were hundreds of Turkic-Mongolian tribes and amongst them were the Oguz, the ancestors of the Turks of Turkey.

In the year 1071, near Manzikert (Manazgird) in Armenia, the Turkic-Mongolian tribes, under the leadership of Alp-Arslan, clashed with the forces of Byzantium. The Emperor of the Holy Roman Empire (Romanus Diogenes) was defeated, and the gates of Asia Minor were opened to the nomadic tribes from Central Asia. 'The Turkic invasion of Anatolia in the eleventh century, and the Ottoman conquest of Constantinople in the fifteenth, brought to completion the assault of Islam on the eastern Roman Empire initiated by the Arabs in the seventh century.'[2]

In the ensuing 850 years those Turkic tribes created and lost a vast empire, based on religion, that in its heyday stretched from the shores of the Atlantic to the Indian Ocean and from the gates of Vienna down to the Red Sea. The Turkish people were saved from eventual oblivion, and no doubt assimilation, by the vision, courage and determination of a great leader, Kemal Atatürk, who by sheer force of character pulled his people from the brink of disaster and literally forced them to enter the twentieth century.

Atatürk created – some say invented – modern Turkey, but the people who first began to change the fabric of a well-established Christian society based on two ancient lineages – that of the Greeks of Asia Minor and the Armenians – were those of the Oguz tribes from the family of Seljuk. The Seljuks were the first Turkic people to settle and establish roots in Asia Minor, with their capital in Konya (ancient Konium) in the heart of Anatolia. Their rule lasted until the beginning of the fourteenth century and was known as the Sultanate of Rum.[3] The sultans were liberal patrons of art and architecture and the remains of the buildings they erected are still amongst the most attractive and interesting in Turkey. The Seljuk Turks were officially Muslim, while the native inhabitants were still Christian and outnumbered the Seljuks, according to William Rubruck, ten to one.[4]

In 1243, near Köse Dāg in Eastern Turkey, the army of the Sultan of Rum was defeated and the hordes of Mongol-Khans plundered their way throughout Asia Minor. The Mongols who destroyed the Seljuk Empire, as well as the Shahs of Persia and the Califs of Baghdad, were too weak to govern the lands they had ravaged. They abandoned the western districts of their empire to the Turkoman lords who, in turn, established the states of Ak Koyunlu, Kara Koyunlu and Ramazan Oğlu. These Turkoman dynasties were later to be vanquished by the Ottoman ruler Muhammed

II 'the Conqueror' in the late fifteenth century. The Ottomans, a dynasty founded by Osman (from whose name derives the word Ottoman) at the beginning of the fourteenth century, established themselves along the shores of the Sea of Marmara and on the Aegean, where they were engaged by land and sea in the Holy War of Islam against the Christian infidels. The Byzantine Empire was finally conquered with the fall of Constantinople in 1453.

In spite of earlier setbacks at the hands of Timur (Tamerlane), the Persian conqueror, the supremacy of the Ottomans was consolidated, and in the reign of Selim I (1512–21), the Ottoman conquest of Asia Minor, Northern Persia and all the Middle Eastern territories of Syria, Egypt, Armenia and Kurdistan was completed. It was left to the sultans who followed Selim, from Suleiman I through to Mahmud II (1803–39), to hold most of these lands, but already by the middle of the eighteenth century the empire had passed its peak.

The Ottomans were not interested in 'trade' as a profession – very much like the ruling aristocracies in England and France of the day. They were born to function as administrators, soldiers or to work on the land. Trade was in the hands of Greeks, Armenians, Jews and Lebanese. 'Much of the overland trade from Persia and the East in Turkey as in Russia was Armenian; there were Armenian as well as Jewish colonies in Leghorn and Marseilles. Greek ship owners . . . already dominated the Black Sea.'[5] Furthermore, the very institutions that had contributed to the strength of Ottoman power also carried within themselves the seeds of their own destruction. The centralisation of power made for efficiency as long as those powers were in strong hands, but they also provided rivalries between the numerous offspring of the Sultans.

From the beginning of the nineteenth century, despite various attempts to endow the Empire with modern structures – army, law, institutions, transport, education and so on – the final agony of decline inexorably set in. Romanians, Bulgarians, Serbians and Greeks liberated themselves, while the Big Powers – Austria, Russia, France and England – quarrelled like hungry vultures in anticipation over the spoils of the Ottoman Empire which, as yet, had not completely been brought to its knees. All attempts at reform failed mainly due to corruption prevailing inside the Court.

In the mid-nineteenth century the movement called 'Young Turks' – an organisation which promoted the concept of a Turkish 'nation' – began to emerge. A 'revolutionary' idea indeed, since for centuries the Empire belonged to one family, that of the Ottomans and their cronies. The populace, and that included the non-Muslims, were merely treated as serfs. At this stage in Turkey's history, two men stood out: Enver Pasha and Mustafa Kemal. The former sought to 'Turkify' all the miscellaneous nationalities of the empire. The latter, though fiercely nationalist, advocated 'westernisation.'

In the First World War, the Young Turks committed a supreme blunder by siding with Germany. After the war the Allies planned to carve up the dead Empire. On October 30, 1918, Sultan Muhammed V capitulated and signed the Armistice of Mudros. Mustafa Kemal rebelled against the conditions of the Armistice which were tantamount to a dismemberment of Turkey. He launched an appeal to his followers and comrades in arms, who joined him and decided to defend Eastern Anatolia at any cost and to expel the Greek army which had been brought into Smyrna (Izmir) by the Allies. This they achieved and in the process virtually burnt down the ancient and magnificent city of Smyrna. Watching the flames of the burning city, Mustafa Kemal proclaimed, in thoughts and language very similar to that of Nero centuries before, 'It is a sign that Turkey is purged of the traitors, the Christians, and of the foreigners, and that Turkey is for the Turks'.[6] Mustafa Kemal became Kemal Atatürk, his new name meaning Father of the Turks.

Religion and society

Atatürk's first priority was to separate the State from the Mosque. He abolished the Califate in 1924. In 1926 legal reforms were inaugurated, based on the Swiss civil code, the Italian penal code and the German commercial code. By 1928 Islam had ceased to be the official religion and the Roman alphabet had replaced the Arabic script.

Turks are ninety-nine per cent Muslim, the majority of whom belong to the Sunni sect. All Muslim law, all social and political institutions of the Ottoman Empire were based on the teachings of the Koran. Kemal Atatürk changed all that – on paper! However, the majority of the population still adheres to many of the laws of Islam, including the dietary laws. Thus, good Muslims do not eat pork or drink intoxicating liquors. They are forbidden to eat or drink from dawn to sunset during the holy month of Ramazan, known as Ramadan in other Muslim countries.

The country

This 'Turkey' of the Turks, a fully-fledged member of the United Nations and a republic, is divided between Europe and Asia with a total area of 296,185 square miles. Generally speaking, Turkey is a dry land. The climate is as rich and varied as its history. It can be divided into four zones; Mediterranean, continental, mountainous and oceanic. Beyond the coastal mountains, the Mediterranean area is rich, lush and fertile.

Here bananas, citrus fruits and sugar thrive. The central Anatolian plateau, which has the mountainous climate, is mostly dry, sparsely populated, rolling steppe, good only for wheat and sheep. It contains Lake Tuz Gölü, the water of which is reputed to be saltier than that of the Dead Sea. In the east of the country, where volcanic activity is rampant, the winters are harsh and summers extremely hot. The Black Sea coastal area on the other hand is temperate, with abundant rainfall and magnificent forests of leaf-bearing and coniferous trees. This region is renowned for its fruit orchards, especially cherries and delicious teas. On the western Aegean coast plentiful rain, mild winters and hot summers have created a rich, well-irrigated region famed for its wheat, cotton, corn, tobacco, grapes and, of course the famous Izmir figs.

The Cuisine

Turkish food is a mirror image of her populace, an amalgam of all the cultures and races that have inhabited the land. In short, the Turkish cuisine is a successful mixture of Europe and Middle East with a little of Central Asia. The people who are proud to call themselves Turks, like many other new nations, such as America, Brazil or Australia, are a mixture of many ethnic groupings and cultures. It is therefore not surprising that Turkish food is so akin to that of Syria and Iraq, Greece and Armenia, for the Turk of today is a direct descendant of Byzantines, Armenians, Kurds, Arabs, Jews, Persians, as well as Hungarians, Albanians and a small percentage of ethnic Turkic-Mongolians from the borders of China.

We must draw a distinction between 'the food of Turkey' and 'Turkish food'. For example, there is a great deal of difference between 'Jewish food' and the 'food of Israel'. We must also note the difference between 'urbanised' and 'provincial' food. Food in general, prepared and served in such major centres as Istanbul, Izmir and to a lesser extent in Ankara, is in reality the food of *Gâvurs* – non-believers, that is Christians. There is little difference between the food in Istanbul and Izmir and, say, Athens or other large cities in Greece. This is particularly true with the fish-based dishes, kebabs, stuffed vegetables and olive oil-based hot and cold dishes.

Similarly, the food of Southern Turkey is like that of Syria and the neighbouring Arab states. The food in Eastern Turkey is strictly of Armenian origin – this region was formerly known as Turkish Armenia. It is in the heart of the land, in Anatolia, that we see 'Turkish' food at its best.

The Muslims of the Ottoman Empire have always eaten well. The Ottoman army was always better organised and better fed than most of its adversaries. The Janissaries – children of non-Muslims who were taken to become 'tribute boys' or slaves of the Sultan and who formed an élite army – had their own military grade of *çorbaji* (literally soup-kitchen sergeants). Corporals were called 'head-cooks' and 'head water-carriers'. The cauldrons in which their *pilavs* and stews were cooked became the equivalent of British regimental colours. None of these warriors was Turkish by origin. Consequently their cooking and food were non-Turkish by origin. The harems were filled with wives, concubines and slaves from all corners of the Empire. They were all of non-'Turkish' origin, and brought with them the culinary specialities of their respective lands and races. No Ottoman Turkish woman, indeed no Muslim woman, could ever be a slave. The latter were either captured during a campaign, bought at a slave market or forcefully dragged from their families. They were all non-Turks too and knew only the food of their non-Turkic-Mongolian mothers. Hence, from the Sultan down to the local district potentate, all the Ottoman dignitaries had non-Ottoman Turkish mothers. Indeed, every Ottoman sultan was by law the son of a 'slave'. The Turkish kitchen has, over the centuries, been enriched by the efforts of those slaves.

What, then, have those slaves left us? They have left a very rich cuisine that can compete with the best in the world. In certain areas it is un-equalled – such as in the rich rice-based *pilav* dishes, or in the use of certain vegetables, particularly aubergines and courgettes, where the Turkish cooks have outdone themselves by creating a vast repertoire as yet untouched by other world cuisines. Similarly, with sweets and desserts – *baklava, tel-kadayif, halva, komposto* and more. Turkish housewives have developed and enlarged the originals which were often Arab, Armenian or Persian. Finally the glory of the Ottoman cuisine; the boregs, originally of Central Asian origin, related to Chinese and Korean dough and rice paper dumplings, have been developed over the ages into a unique art form. They have transcended the boundaries of Anatolia and have spread throughout North Africa, the Balkans and the Middle East.

Turkish food, however, is still Middle Eastern food. The optimum use of lamb, the complete absence of pork, the non-existence of alcohol (both in food and on the dinner table), and also the great use and love of sweetmeats, yogurt, fruit drinks, tea and coffee are all characteristics of other Middle Eastern lands. Turkish food in general is not hot or spicy, particularly in the western regions of the country. Turks do use spices and herbs carefully and cleverly, but not with abandon as, say, the people of the Indian sub-continent. The favourite herbs and spices are dill, tarragon, rosemary, thyme, marjoram, cinnamon and allspice. The favourite nuts are almonds, pistachios and pine kernels and they are used in soups, stews, sauces, stuffings, *pilavs* and, of course in the sugary pastries which are sold in the aromatic patisseries of Istanbul and Ankara.

Visitors' Turkey

Tourism in Turkey is still in its infancy. It lags behind all other European countries. Throughout the land, service, quality and availability of goods and comforts are still inadequate to satisfy a discriminating Westerner; but tourism in general is making big strides. Standards are rapidly rising and it is only a matter of time, a decade or two, before Turkey becomes a major tourist centre.

Until the early Eighties tourism was not taken seriously by the Turks. Matters have now changed and there is a government-sponsored push to make maximum use of the wealth of attractions in the country. To achieve this goal much has to change, for many travellers have in recent times returned from Turkey very disappointed. Hotels are fast appearing, and money-earning 'western colonies' are being developed near such ancient towns as Bodrum, Marmaris, Altin Kum, Olu Deniz and particularly along the magnificent coastline of ancient Antalya and Alanya. Similarly, on the Black Sea coastline, new purpose-built hotels, offering all expected facilities have been rapidly erected in expectation of the forthcoming tourist onslaught.

But outside these holiday bases life in the real Turkey goes on as it has done for centuries. The muezzin's chants mingle with the bray of donkeys, the roar of traffic, the clatter and chatter of people who are content with life and not envious of other folk's possessions. In the cafés men will sip tea, black coffee or *ayran,* the ubiquitous yogurt drink, and discuss politics. Young people will be drinking cool, refreshing fruit juices or licking *dondurma* (ice cream) flavoured with mastic, that is hung like an animal carcass from the ceiling of the ice cream shop. The bazaars, large or small, will be a wealth of colour, flavour and texture, the sun will be shining, birds singing, and people smiling. And you, a stranger, a passerby through their land must appreciate and respect their culture which in many ways is totally different from yours.

Always be prepared to read a little about the country you plan to visit.

Find out about the people and culture. Learn a smattering of the language and, above all, about the social and religious laws and conventions. There is nothing like the broad smile on a Turk's face when a foreigner salutes him or her with a few well-chosen words of his or her mother tongue.

For those who wish to know more about Turkey I suggest the following books:

HISTORY AND PERSONALITIES
The Turks of Central Asia M. A. Czatlicka
  London 1918
Atatürk, the Rebirth of a Nation
  Lord Kinross 1964
The March of the Barbarians
  Harold Lamb 1941
Suleiman the Magnificent Harold Lamb 1941
The Old Turkey and the New
  Sir Harry Luke 1953
Turkey Andrew Mango 1968
In the Days of the Janissaries
  Alexander Pallis 1955
The Rise of the Ottoman Empire
  Paul Wittek 1938

TRAVEL
Aegean Turkey George E. Bean 1966
Turkey's Southern Shore George E. Bean 1960
Riding to the Tigris Freya Stark 1959
Ionia; a Quest Freya Stark 1954
East of Trabizond Michael Pereira 1971
Turkish Panorama Stowers Johnson 1968
By Road to Turkey Robert Bell 1962
Journey into the Sunrise John Marriner 1970
Unknown Turkey Georges Pilimant 1974
Alexander's Path from Caria to Cilicia
  Freya Stark 1958
Eastern Turkey Gwyn Williams 1972

Finally, I must say a few words about 'The Hodja', the wit, philosopher, lawyer and scholar who lived in the thirteenth century. Nasurettin Hodja was born in Sivrihisar in Central Turkey and died in Eskiçehir. He was a simple, happy person who was satisfied with his lot and always tried to make others happy. He mocked the pretentious and loved justice and the weak. His tomb, a large stone, has walls that are covered with graffiti by thousands of admirers from all generations. The wit of the Hodja is the wit of the entire Middle East. The thousands of years of social, economic, religious and, above all, human development have been synthesised in the name and words of a wise, learned man who lived in the turmoil-ridden Middle Ages.

I have used several stories and homilies of his which, in one form or another, are related to food.

NOTES
[1] *The Emergence of Modern Turkey* Bernard Lewis. Oxford University 1961.
[2] *A History of the Ottoman Empire to 1730* Ed. M. A. Cook. Cambridge University Press 1976.
[3] The name *Rum* is the Arabic for Rome; hence their descendants the Byzantines and, through them, the Seljuks of Konya.
[4] *Pre-Ottoman Turkey* Claude Cahen. Translation J. Jones-Williams. Sidgwick & Jackson 1968.
[5] *A History of the Ottoman Empire* (op. cit.).
[6] *Lords of the Golden Horns.* Noel Barber. Macmillan 1973.

CHAPTER ONE

MEZELER
Hors d'oeuvre

'*A man does not eat what he desires,*
but what he finds.'
KURDISH SÁYING

In the small *lokantas* (restaurants) of Istanbul, Izmir and, to a lesser extent Ankara, the chefs will fill your table with countless small plates filled to the brim with tit-bits of all sorts. The list will contain different kinds and colours of olives, cheeses, roasted nuts (almonds, pistachios, peanuts, hazelnuts), fried whitebait, sardines, anchovies, meatballs, slices of *pastirma*, all kinds of fresh vegetables, small boregs, stuffed vine leaves, salads made with fruits, beans, aubergines, courgettes, tomatoes and, of course, *turşu* (pickles). The waiters, with a little prompting, will refill the empty plates while at one end of the restaurant the chefs will be cooking the fish or meat kebabs. All this and heaven too!

One of the most endearing features of the Turkish cuisine is the sumptuous *mezeler* (hors d'oeuvre) table. In typical Middle Eastern style, the *meze* tables often surpassed, both in quantity and quality, the courses that followed it. The Kurdish saying quoted above reveals that Turks may not be able to eat what they desire all of the time, but the Turkish housewife, from the often limited raw material available concocts variation upon variation of delicious and appetising dishes, so that 'what he desires' and 'what he finds' must often coincide. A few dishes are included below.

NAZKATUN
Aubergine Dip
———— · ● · ————

One of the countless aubergine dips popular throughout the Middle East and the Balkans. This recipe, however, is different in that as well as the standard yogurt or *tahina* (see Glossary), it also incorporates pomegranate juice and toasted almonds. If fresh pomegranates are not available, the concentrated syrup can be bought at Middle Eastern stores. (See Glossary.) Serve with bread and pickles.

3 large aubergines
300 ml (½ pint) yogurt
22.5 ml (1½ tablespoons) pomegranate
  juice *or* lemon juice *or* 10 ml
  (2 teaspoons) concentrated
  pomegranate syrup
2.5 ml (½ teaspoon) salt

5 ml (1 teaspoon) dried mint
50 g (2 oz) toasted almonds, finely
  chopped
Garnish
30 ml (2 tablespoons) parsley or
  tarragon, finely chopped

Make 2 or 3 slits in each aubergine and then cook over charcoal, under a hot grill or in a hot oven until the skins are black and the flesh feels soft when poked with a finger. When cool enough to handle peel away the skins, scraping off and reserving any flesh which comes away with the skin.

Cut the flesh into small pieces and place in a bowl. Mash them with a fork and then add all the remaining ingredients. Mix thoroughly and then set aside to cool.

When ready to serve spread the purée over a large plate and garnish with the fresh herbs.

HÜNKÂR BEĞENDI
Aubergine Purée with Cheese
———— · ● · ————

This variation of the above aubergine dish is eaten as a dip or as a side dish with kebabs. The name means 'the king liked it' – and so he should have, it is very tasty!

3 large aubergines
25 ml (1½ tablespoons) lemon juice
25 g (1 oz) butter
30 ml (2 tablespoons) flour
90 ml (6 tablespoons) hot milk

100 g (4 oz) crumbled feta *or* grated
  cheddar
5 ml (1 teaspoon) salt
2.5 ml (½ teaspoon) chilli pepper

Prepare the aubergines as described above.

Place the flesh in a saucepan and mash with a fork. Add the lemon juice and cook over a low heat for 5 minutes, stirring frequently.

Meanwhile in another small pan melt the butter. Add the flour and cook for about 5 minutes until it is golden, stirring constantly. Stir this mixture into the aubergines and then gradually add the milk, stirring constantly until the mixture is creamy.

Add the cheese, salt and pepper and cook for 2 more minutes until the mixture forms a thick purée.

BAKLA

Broad Beans in Oil

'BAKLA –
to see – love, care
dried version – argument, disagreement
to cook – help the poor, but not appreciated
to eat – argument, sickness
to eat it raw – carelessness
to buy – poverty, have problems of the heart
to sell – to bring trouble to others.'

from a 19TH-CENTURY BOOK OF DREAMS

———— • ● • ————

Despite the above this is one of Turkey's most popular salads which is often also eaten as a main meal with the accompaniment of a rice *pilav*.

As always yogurt accompanies these Turkish salad dishes, but I think a yogurt-garlic sauce is more successful with this salad (see *Samersakli Yogurt* p. 92).

900 g (2 lb) broad bean pods, washed and stringed
juice of 1 lemon
5 ml (1 teaspoon) salt
4–5 vine leaves or large cabbage leaves
4–5 spring onions, cut into 1-cm (½-inch) pieces
30 ml (2 tablespoons) chopped fresh mint *or* 15 ml (1 tablespoon) dried mint
30 ml (2 tablespoons) chopped fresh dill *or* 15 ml (1 tablespoon) dried dillweed
2.5 ml (½ teaspoon) allspice
360 ml (12 fl oz) water
120 ml (4 fl oz) olive oil
Garnish
15 ml (1 tablespoon) parsley, finely chopped

Put the washed beans in a large bowl, add the lemon juice and salt, toss and leave for 15 minutes.

Meanwhile, line the bottom of a large saucepan with vine leaves or some cabbage leaves. Cover the leaves with half the beans. Sprinkle the spring onions, mint and dill evenly over the beans and then lay the remaining beans over the top. Sprinkle over the allspice and then pour in the water and oil.

Cover the pan and place over a medium to low heat and cook for about 1–1½ hours or until the beans are tender. Remove from the heat and set aside to cool.

When the beans are cold transfer them to a serving dish and sprinkle with the parsley. Serve with plain yogurt or a yogurt-garlic sauce.

ÇILBIR

Egg on Toast with Spiced Yogurt

'Even his cock lays eggs.'
– Such a lucky fellow!

———— • ● • ————

This is a traditional Turkish recipe which makes an excellent savoury snack.

40 g (1½ oz) butter
6 eggs
6 large rounds of toast
300 ml (½ pint) yogurt
5 ml (level teaspoon) salt

2.5 ml (½ teaspoon) freshly ground
  black pepper
2.5 ml (½ teaspoon) ground cumin
25 g (1 oz) butter, melted
5 ml (1 teaspoon) paprika

Melt the 40 g (1½ oz) butter in a large frying pan and break the eggs in gently. Cook until just firm.

Meanwhile arrange the rounds of toast on a large platter. Place 1 egg on top of each slice of toast.

Beat the yogurt with the salt, pepper and cumin until creamy. Pour this mixture over the eggs.

Mix the melted butter and paprika together and spoon over the eggs. Serve immediately.

KIYMALI YUMURTA

Egg and Meat Omelette

———— • ● • ————

A quick, simple and filling dish. It also makes an ideal lunch if served with a bowl of salad, bread and home-made pickles.

You can add 100 g (4 oz) spinach or purslane to give the dish more substance.

25 g (1 oz) butter
1 small onion, skinned and finely
  chopped
1 garlic clove, skinned and crushed
450 g (1 lb) minced lamb *or* beef
30 ml (2 tablespoons) parsley or
  coriander, finely chopped
15 ml (1 tablespoon) tomato purée

60 ml (4 tablespoons) water
5 ml (1 teaspoon) salt
1.25 ml (¼ teaspoon) black pepper
6 large eggs
Garnish
2.5 ml (½ teaspoon) paprika
2.5 ml (½ teaspoon) cumin

Melt the butter in a large frying pan, add the onion and garlic and fry for 3 minutes, stirring regularly. Add the minced meat and fry for 5 minutes or until nicely browned, stirring with a wooden spoon to break down the lumps. Stir in the parsley or coriander, tomato purée, water, salt and pepper. Cover the pan and simmer for about 20 minutes or until the meat is cooked.

Uncover the pan and break the eggs over the mixture, spacing them evenly. Cover and cook for a further 5 minutes or until the eggs are firm. Serve with a little paprika and cumin sprinkled over each portion.

YALANÇI DOLMASI
Vine Leaves Stuffed with Rice

'Eat the grapes, don't ask about the vineyard.'
– Do something without asking too many questions.

———— ·•· ————

This is a classic of the Middle Eastern cuisine which is particularly popular in Turkey, Armenia, Greece, Syria and Lebanon.

The idea of stuffing vegetables and leaves is a very old one and, most probably, of Anatolian origin dating back to the ancient Hittites and Urartians.

There are several popular fillings, three of which are given below, and although the cooking method is the same the sauces vary.

By far the most oriental of the versions is the Armenian, while the Istanbul version is more sophisticated and less spicy.

350 g (¾ lb) vine leaves

Filling 1 – Armenian version
150 ml (¼ pint) olive oil
2 onions, skinned and thinly sliced
1 green pepper, seeded and thinly sliced
175 g (6 oz) long grain rice, washed thoroughly under cold water and drained
2.5 ml (½ teaspoon) chilli pepper
5 ml (1 teaspoon) allspice
5 ml (1 teaspoon) salt
22.5 ml (1½ tablespoons) tomato purée
25 g (1 oz) chopped almonds
15 ml (1 tablespoon) parsley, finely chopped

Filling 2 – Anatolian version
150 ml (¼ pint) olive oil
2 onions, skinned and thinly sliced
175 g (6 oz) long grain rice, washed thoroughly under cold water and drained
25 g (1 oz) pine kernels
25 g (1 oz) sultanas
5 ml (1 teaspoon) salt
5 ml (1 teaspoon) sugar
2.5 ml (½ teaspoon) cinnamon
2.5 ml (½ teaspoon) freshly ground black pepper
10 ml (2 teaspoons) allspice
15 ml (1 tablespoon) parsley, finely chopped

Filling 3 – Istanbul version
150 ml (¼ pint) olive oil
175 g (6 oz) long grain rice, washed thoroughly under cold water and drained
25 g (1 oz) pine kernels
25 g (1 oz) sultanas
30 ml (2 tablespoons) sugar
5 ml (1 teaspoon) dried dillweed or
    15 ml (1 tablespoon) chopped fresh dill
10 ml (2 teaspoons) allspice
1.25 ml (¼ teaspoon) cinnamon

Sauce for Filling 1
15 ml (1 tablespoon) tomato purée
1.2–1.8 litres (2–3 pints) water
4 garlic cloves, skinned and crushed
5 ml (1 teaspoon) salt
2.5 ml (½ teaspoon) chilli pepper
45 ml (3 tablespoons) lemon juice

Sauce for Fillings 2 and 3
1.2–1.8 litres (2–3 pints) water
juice of ½ lemon

Wash the leaves in cold water, place them in a saucepan, cover with water and bring to the boil. Simmer for 15 minutes and then drain into a colander.

To prepare Filling 1: heat the oil in a large saucepan, add the sliced onions and green peppers and fry for 5–10 minutes, stirring occasionally until the onions are soft but not brown. Add the rice, pepper, allspice, salt and tomato purée and cook gently, stirring frequently to prevent sticking, for about 10 minutes. Remove the pan from the heat and stir in the almonds and parsley.

To prepare Filling 2: heat the oil in a large saucepan, add the onions and fry for 5–10 minutes until the onions are soft but not brown. Add the rice and all the remaining ingredients except the parsley and cook gently for about 10 minutes, stirring frequently to prevent sticking. Remove from the heat and stir in the parsley.

To prepare Filling 3: heat the oil in a large saucepan, add all the remaining ingredients and cook gently for about 10 minutes, stirring frequently to prevent sticking.

When the filling of your choice is cooked turn it into a bowl and leave to cool. To make each *dolma* follow the diagrams below.

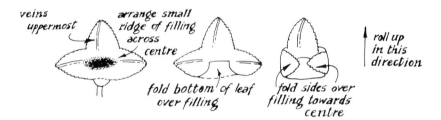

Continue in this way until you have used all the filling.

Cover the bottom of a saucepan with any remaining or broken vine leaves – this will help to prevent the bottom of the pan burning. Pack the *dolmas* carefully and closely in the saucepan in layers. Put a plate over the top of the *dolmas* and hold it down with a weight – this will prevent the *dolmas* from moving and coming apart during cooking.

Mix the ingredients for whichever sauce you are using together and pour into the saucepan making sure that the *dolmas* are completely covered. Add more water if necessary. Bring to the boil, lower the heat and simmer for 1½–2 hours.

Remove from the heat, take off the weight and plate and remove 1 *dolma* to test if the leaf is tender. If so, set the pan aside to cool.

When cool, remove the *dolmas* from the pan and arrange on a serving plate. Serve with fresh yogurt or lemon wedges.

ARNAVUT CİĞERİ
Albanian Liver

Where is my cat?
Nasurettin Hodja was very fond of liver, and
so was his wife. Indeed, every time he brought
some home his wife would seize the
opportunity, grill or make a kebab of it, invite
her friends and give a party. Come evening
and the Hodja would again be fed a little soup
or rice pilav. The excuse would always be the same:
'That miserable cat must have stolen the liver.'
On one such night the Hodja could stand it no more.
He sprang up, rushed to his neighbour's house and
borrowed his weighing machine. He tied a
handkerchief around the cat's middle and weighed
carefully. Then turning to his bewildered wife:
'I thought so!' he exclaimed, his cheeks all red. 'The liver
I brought home this morning weighed exactly one kilo.
Now this cat weighs exactly one kilo too.
Well woman, tell me in God's name, if this be the
liver where the hell is my cat?'

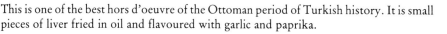

This is one of the best hors d'oeuvre of the Ottoman period of Turkish history. It is small pieces of liver fried in oil and flavoured with garlic and paprika.

1 onion, skinned and thinly sliced, *or*
  6 spring onions, sliced into thin rings
450 g (1 lb) lambs' liver, gristle removed
30 ml (2 tablespoons) flour
15 ml (1 tablespoon) paprika

60 ml (4 tablespoons) olive oil
2 garlic cloves, skinned and crushed
Garnish
30 ml (2 tablespoons) parsley, finely
  chopped

Arrange the sliced onion over a serving plate.

Wash the liver and pat dry. Cut into 2-cm (¾-inch) pieces.

Place the flour and half the paprika in a bowl and mix well. Add the liver pieces and toss until well coated.

Heat the oil in a frying pan, add the liver pieces and fry for 2–3 minutes, turning once or twice. Do not overcook. The pieces of meat should still be pink and juicy inside. Remove the liver with a slotted spoon and arrange on the onion slices.

Pour off all but 45 ml (3 tablespoons) of the oil. Add the remaining paprika and the garlic to the pan and fry for 1 minute, stirring constantly. Pour this paprika-oil mixture over the liver and set aside to cool. Garnish with parsley and serve.

IMAM BAYILDI

Stuffed Aubergines in Olive Oil

*'You might as well expect tears from the dead,
as a decent meal from an Imam.'*

———— • • • ————

One of the great classics of Turkish cooking, this dish of aubergines stuffed with onions, tomatoes and green peppers has entered the repertoire of international cuisine. There is a certain mystique about this dish, with several nationalities claiming it as theirs. It is also claimed to be good for one's liver and digestion. The truth of the matter is that this is a magnificent dish worthy of the Imam (Muslim priest) who, allegedly, fainted at the sight of all the olive oil used. Traditionally in the Middle East all savoury dishes to be eaten cold are made with olive oil, but this can make the dish rather heavy for western tastes – as well as expensive – and there is no reason why you cannot use a lighter oil instead. Serve with bread.

6 medium aubergines
120 ml (8 tablespoons) olive oil
3 onions, skinned and thinly sliced
3 green peppers, thinly sliced
3 garlic cloves, skinned and coarsely chopped
3 ripe tomatoes, thinly sliced
45 ml (3 tablespoons) tomato purée

10 ml (2 teaspoons) salt
5 ml (1 teaspoon) allspice
5 ml (1 teaspoon) paprika
45 ml (3 tablespoons) finely chopped parsley
300 ml (½ pint) olive oil or lighter oil
600 ml (1 pint) boiling water

Wash and dry the aubergines, leaving on the stalks. Make a slit about 2.5–5 cm (1–2 inches) long down each aubergine. Sprinkle salt inside the slits and set aside for 15 minutes.

Meanwhile, heat the 120 ml (8 tablespoons) of olive oil in a large saucepan, add the onions, green peppers and garlic and fry gently for about 10 minutes. Add the tomatoes, tomato purée, salt, allspice and paprika and cook for a further 5 minutes. Stir in half the parsley and remove from the heat.

Rinse out the aubergines and pat dry with kitchen paper.

Heat the 300 ml (½ pint) oil in a large frying pan and fry the aubergines, turning a few times, until the flesh begins to soften. Remove the aubergines and arrange, side by side, in an ovenproof dish, slit sides uppermost.

Carefully prise open the slits and spoon the onion mixture into each slit. If there is any onion mixture left, add this to the dish and then pour in the boiling water. Place in the centre of an oven preheated to 200°C (400°F) gas mark 6 and cook for 1 hour.

Remove from the oven, let cool and then refrigerate. Before serving, garnish with the remaining parsley.

MEZELIK KÖFTELER
Small meatballs
· ● ·

These spicy little meatballs are served cold and make excellent appetisers. They are also ideal to serve as part of a buffet. Accompany with gherkins, olives, lemon wedges, radishes and sliced tomatoes.

900 g (2 lb) lean lamb, minced twice	5 ml (1 teaspoon) allspice
10 ml (2 teaspoons) salt	3 garlic cloves, skinned and crushed
5 ml (1 teaspoon) black pepper	2 eggs
5 ml (1 teaspoon) cumin	150 ml (¼ pint) oil

Place the minced meat in a large bowl and knead with your hands for a few minutes. Add the salt, pepper, cumin, allspice and crushed garlic and knead until well blended. Break the eggs into the mixture and continue to knead until really smooth. Refrigerate for several hours.

When ready to cook remove the meat from the refrigerator and dampen your hands. Form the mixture into marble-sized balls. It helps to keep your palms damp while doing this.

Heat the oil in a frying pan and fry some of the balls for about 10 minutes or until cooked through and evenly browned. Remove with a slotted spoon and transfer to a serving dish. Continue cooking the meatballs in this way. Add more oil if necessary. Leave to cool and then serve.

ÇERKEZ TAVUĞU
Circassian Chicken
· ● ·

This chicken in walnut sauce is one of the great Georgian specialities which is also popular throughout Turkey. It is simply delicious and it is unfortunate that the Caucasian cuisine is perhaps the least known of all the Middle Eastern cuisines. It can be served cold as an appetiser (as here) or warm as a main dish.

1.5 kg (3 lb) chicken, quartered	*Garnish*
1 onion, skinned and coarsely chopped	15 ml (1 tablespoon) olive oil
1 carrot, peeled and cut into rings	5 ml (1 teaspoon) paprika
175 g (6 oz) walnuts	15 ml (1 tablespoon) parsley, finely
2 thick slices white bread	chopped
5 ml (1 teaspoon) salt	15 ml (1 tablespoon) tarragon, finely
2.5 ml (½ teaspoon) freshly ground	chopped
black pepper	

Place the chicken pieces in a large saucepan, cover with water, add the onion, carrot and a pinch of salt and bring to the boil. Lower the heat and simmer for about 45 minutes or until the chicken is tender.

Transfer the chicken pieces to a plate and, when cool enough to handle, discard the skin and strip the flesh from the bones. Return the bones to the stock and simmer until the stock is reduced.

Cut the chicken into strips about 5 cm (2 inches) long and 1 cm (½ inch) thick.

Grind the walnuts and bread in a blender and turn into a saucepan. Slowly stir in some of the stock until you have a smooth paste. Season with the salt and pepper. If the sauce is too thin, simmer over a low heat until it thickens.

Put the paprika and oil in a small bowl and set aside.

If serving as an appetiser pile the shredded chicken on to a serving dish and spoon the sauce over the top. Set aside to cool.

If serving hot then add the strips of chicken to the sauce and heat through thoroughly before piling into a serving dish.

Just before serving dribble the oil-paprika mixture over the chicken and sprinkle with the parsley and tarragon.

PATATES KÖFTESI
Potato Balls
—— • ● • ——

These are small balls of mashed potatoes stuffed with a minced meat mixture and then fried in oil. They are delicious and make excellent appetisers. Served accompanied by salads they also make an ideal lunch or supper dish.

6 medium potatoes
1 egg
2.5 ml (½ teaspoon) salt
1.25 ml (¼ teaspoon) freshly ground
   black pepper
1.25 ml (¼ teaspoon) allspice
Stuffing
25 g (1 oz) butter
1 onion, finely chopped
225 g (½ lb) minced lamb

2 tomatoes, blanched, peeled and
   chopped
2 cloves of garlic, finely chopped
2.5 ml (½ teaspoon) salt
2.5 ml (½ teaspoon) paprika
To fry
2 eggs
oil
To serve
lettuce leaves

Peel the potatoes, boil until tender, drain and mash. When cool add the egg, salt, black pepper and allspice and mix until well blended and smooth.

Prepare the stuffing by melting the butter in a small pan and frying the onion until soft. Add the meat, tomatoes, garlic, salt and paprika and fry gently until the meat is cooked and the mixture is dry. Leave to cool.

Using a tablespoon take out enough of the potato mixture to make, with your hands, a patty about 5 cm (2 inches) in diameter. Place 5 ml (1 teaspoon) of the meat mixture in the centre of the patty and then mould the potato mixture around the filling to enclose it and form a ball. Roll it between your palms until it is smooth. Repeat this process until all the potato and meat mixtures have been used.

Heat some oil in a large frying pan.

Beat the 2 eggs in a bowl and then dip the potato balls, one at a time, into them.

Fry a few at a time, turning frequently until they are golden on all sides. Remove with a slotted spoon, drain on kitchen paper and then arrange on a bed of lettuce leaves. Serve hot.

SARDALYA TAVASI
Fried Sardines
— • ● • —

Near Istanbul's Egyptian Bazaar are found most of the fish, spice and flower markets with countless stalls vying with each other. There are fish-boat restaurants moored to the quayside and the stalls display freshly landed fish such as tunny, mackerel, bass, swordfish and, one of Istanbul's favourites, sardines, caught in the Sea of Marmara. They are often just cleaned, tossed in flour, fried in oil and eaten with a few drops of lemon juice. This way they are simply delicious.

BARBUNYA PLAKISI
Fish Plaki
— • ● • —

This dish is loved by the Turks, Greeks and Armenians and they all claim to have originated it. Turks love to use *barbunya* (red mullet), but halibut or any meaty white fish will do as well. This dish also makes an excellent fish course or light lunch.

6 pieces fish, approx 175 g (6 oz) each, e.g. halibut, mullet, bass
6 medium carrots, peeled and sliced
6 sticks celery, cut into 2.5-cm (1-inch) pieces
1 onion, skinned and thinly sliced
1 large green pepper, cut into 12 pieces
3 large potatoes, peeled and cut into 1-cm (½-inch) thick slices
120 ml (8 tablespoons) olive oil

3 garlic cloves, skinned and crushed
30 ml (2 tablespoons) tomato purée
7.5 ml (1½ teaspoons) salt
2.5 ml (½ teaspoon) chilli pepper
900 ml (1½ pints) water

Garnish
lemon wedges
30 ml (2 tablespoons) parsley, finely chopped

Place all the vegetables in a large colander and wash thoroughly under cold running water. Drain well.

Heat the oil in a large saucepan, add the vegetables, stir well, cover and cook over a moderate heat for about 30 minutes, shaking the pan occasionally.

Meanwhile brush the base of a large ovenproof dish with a little oil and arrange the fish in it. Preheat the oven to 200°C (400°F) gas mark 6.

After the allotted 30 minutes remove the saucepan from the heat and, with a slotted spoon remove the vegetables carefully and arrange over the fish.

Return the saucepan to the fire and heat up any oil that remains. Add the garlic and fry for 1 minute. Stir in the tomato purée, salt and pepper and cook gently for a further 3 minutes. Add the water and bring to the boil. Pour this sauce over the vegetables, place the dish in the oven and cook for about 45 minutes or until the fish is tender. Remove from the oven and set aside to cool.

Arrange the pieces of fish on a serving plate and spoon the vegetables and sauce over the top. Garnish with the lemon wedges and parsley.

SARDALYA SARMASI
Sardines in Vine Leaves

———— • ● • ————

This is another popular treatment of sardines. The sardines are washed, cleaned, heads and tails are removed and then each one is wrapped in a vine leaf which is well rubbed with olive oil.

Some olive oil is heated in a pan until sizzling hot and then the *sarmas* are fried, a few at a time, for 2–3 minutes until crisp on each side.

Serve with lemon juice and pickled cucumbers.

USKUMRU PILÂKISI
Mackerel in Olive Oil

'He always floats like olive oil.'
– He always comes off best.

———— • ● • ————

Turks love mackerel more than any other fish except *barbunya* (red mullet). They pickle it in salt, mince it for soup balls, fry it, stuff it and also cook it in olive oil as with this famous dish, a favourite of Armenians as well as Turks.

A good Muslim will naturally not use wine, but this recipe appears to be for those who value their palates more than the salvation of their souls!

6 medium mackerel	22.5 ml (1½ tablespoons) tomato purée
300 ml (½ pint) olive oil	150 ml (¼ pint) dry white wine
4 onions, skinned and thinly sliced	750 ml (1¼ pints) fish stock or water
5 garlic cloves, skinned and halved	**Garnish**
3 carrots, peeled and thinly sliced	30 ml (2 tablespoons) parsley, finely
5 ml (1 teaspoon) salt	chopped
5 ml (1 teaspoon) chilli pepper	

Scale and clean the insides of the fish, but do not cut off the heads and tails.

Heat half the oil in a large frying pan. Add the onions, garlic and carrots and cook over a low heat for about 10 minutes.

Add the remaining oil, salt, pepper, tomato purée, wine and stock, stir well and bring gently to the boil. Cover the pan and simmer for 20 minutes.

Remove the pan from the heat and strain the contents into a sieve, collecting the liquid in a bowl. Discard the vegetables.

Arrange the mackerel side by side in a large pan and pour in the liquid. Cover the pan and bring gently to the boil. Simmer for 20–30 minutes or until the fish are tender. Turn off the heat and set aside to cool.

Place the fish in a large serving dish, pour the sauce over the top, sprinkle with the parsley and serve.

CHAPTER TWO

PILAVLAR
Pilavs

'Every hero will eat pilav in his own way.'
– Everyone will think and react in his own style.

Rice is the staple diet of the Turks. In their original homelands bordering on China and Mongolia their diet consisted of mare's milk, animal blood and rice. Consequently Turkish cooks are masters of rice dishes. Over the centuries they have created many attractive and tasty rice-based recipes making great use of local ingredients, herbs, spices, nuts, fruits and vegetables. Although not as exuberant and lavish as many of the Iranian *pilavs* the Turks do have some of the finest *pilav* dishes in the world.

Plain rice *pilav* is the most popular of all and is served daily all over the land as an accompaniment to a dish of kebabs, a rich vegetable stew or as a quick snack topped with a little yogurt. This is closely followed by *Melek Pilavi* – vermicelli *pilav* – which is often served to the sick and the young. Other grains are also used to make *pilavs* such as burghul (cracked wheat), whole wheat or barley, but it is to the rice grain that the Anatolian housewife turns most often and on which she lavishes her care and artistry. Any sort of long grain rice can be used, the best results being achieved with basmati rice.

PIRINÇ PILAVI
Plain Rice Pilav
———— • ● • ————

50 g (2 oz) butter or *ghee*
350 g (12 oz) long grain rice, washed thoroughly under cold running water and drained

5 ml (1 teaspoon) salt
900 ml (1½ pints) meat or vegetable stock or water, boiling

Melt the butter or *ghee* in a large saucepan. Add the drained rice and fry for a few minutes, stirring frequently. Add the salt and stock or water and bring back to the boil. Allow to boil vigorously for 3 minutes and then, lower the heat, cover and simmer for 15–20 minutes or until all the liquid has been absorbed.

Turn off the heat, remove the lid, cover the top of the pan with a tea towel, replace the lid and leave to 'rest' for 10–15 minutes.

Fluff up the rice with a long-pronged fork and serve.

DOMATESLI PILAVI
Tomato Pilav

'Anyone who refuses his Pilav, let his spoon break.'
– Anyone who breaks his promise is a coward.
———— • ● • ————

This is an extremely popular *pilav* in Turkey which can be served with all kinds of meat dishes.

50 g (2 oz) butter or *ghee*
1 onion, skinned and thinly sliced
450 g (1 lb) tomatoes, blanched, peeled and chopped
1 garlic clove, skinned and crushed
2.5 ml (½ teaspoon) dried basil
45 ml (3 tablespoons) parsley, finely chopped

5 ml (1 teaspoon) salt
2.5 ml (½ teaspoon) freshly ground black pepper
350 g (12 oz) long grain rice, washed thoroughly under cold running water and drained
900 ml (1½ pints) water or meat or vegetable stock, boiling

Melt the butter or *ghee* in a large saucepan. Add the onion and fry for 5–10 minutes until soft, but not brown. Add the tomatoes, garlic, basil, parsley, salt and pepper and fry for 3–4 minutes, stirring frequently. Add the rice and mix well.

Stir in the water or stock and boil vigorously for 3 minutes. Lower the heat, cover the pan and simmer for 15–20 minutes or until the liquid has been absorbed.

Turn off the heat, remove the lid, cover the pan with a tea towel and replace the lid. Leave the *pilav* to 'rest' for 10–15 minutes and then fluff up with a long-pronged fork and serve.

ISTANBUL PILAVI
Chicken, Saffron and Nut Pilav
———— • • • ————

This is a delightful rice *pilav* with chicken and nuts. It is delicately flavoured with saffron which also gives it an attractive pinkish colour. It often accompanies roast or kebab dishes, but it can be served on its own with yogurt and/or a salad.

50 g (2 oz) butter or *ghee*

2 cooked chicken breasts, flesh cut into 1-cm (½-inch) pieces

60 ml (4 tablespoons) blanched almonds, either halved or slivered

60 ml (4 tablespoons) pistachio nuts, halved

350g (12 oz) long grain rice, rinsed under cold water and drained

5 ml (1 teaspoon) salt

2.5 ml (½ teaspoon) freshly ground black pepper

1.25 ml (¼ teaspoon) crushed saffron strands, soaked in 30 ml (2 tablespoons) boiling water for 20 minutes

900 ml (1½ pints) meat or vegetable stock or water, boiling

Melt the butter or *ghee* in a large saucepan, add the nuts and lightly fry for 2 minutes, stirring constantly. Add the chicken pieces, and fry for a further 2–3 minutes, stirring frequently. Remove the nuts and chicken pieces with a slotted spoon and reserve.

Add the rice, salt and pepper to the pan and fry for 2–3 minutes, stirring frequently. Add the saffrom mixture and the boiling water or stock. Allow to boil vigorously for 3 minutes and then lower the heat, cover the pan and simmer for 15–20 minutes or until the liquid is absorbed. Ten minutes before the end of the cooking time, stir in the chicken mixture, re-cover and continue cooking.

Turn off the heat, remove the lid, cover the pan with a tea towel, replace the lid and leave to 'rest' for 10–15 minutes.

Fluff up with a long-pronged fork, turn into a large dish and serve.

SULTAN REŞAT PILAVI
Aubergine Pilav
———— • • • ————

This is named after one of the Ottoman sultans who reigned about 1786 and who must have been rather partial to aubergines. This is a magnificent rice *pilav* which goes well with all kinds of meat and poultry dishes.

3 large aubergines, peeled

75 g (3 oz) butter or *ghee*

1 large onion, skinned and roughly chopped

3 large tomatoes, blanched, peeled and chopped

50 g (2 oz) vermicelli, broken into 2.5-cm (1-inch) pieces

7.5 ml (1½ teaspoons) salt

2.5 ml (½ teaspoon) freshly ground black pepper

250 g (9 oz) long grain rice, washed thoroughly under cold water and drained

a few mint leaves

900 ml (1½ pints) meat or vegetable stock, boiling

Cut the aubergines into 1-cm (½-inch) cubes. Place in a colander, sprinkle with salt and set aside for 20–30 minutes.

Meanwhile melt the butter or *ghee* in a large saucepan. Add the onion and fry for a few minutes until it is soft, but do not let it brown. Stir in the tomatoes, vermicelli, salt and pepper and fry for 2–3 minutes.

Rinse the aubergines thoroughly, dry them on kitchen paper and add to the pan. Fry, stirring constantly, for 3–4 minutes. Stir in the rice, mint leaves and boiling stock and bring back to the boil. Lower the heat and simmer for about 20 minutes or until the liquid is absorbed and the rice is tender.

Turn off the heat, cover the pan with a tea towel and set aside to 'rest' for 10–15 minutes. Fluff up with a long-pronged fork and serve.

HELP YOURSELF, MY FUR COAT

*One day the Hodja was invited to a wedding.
Having arrived in his usual shabby attire he realised
that no one seemed to take any notice of him. He was
simply ignored, humiliated and had to stand well back in
the corner of the room. Well, this wouldn't do for
our Hodja. So he quietly slipped out. When he arrived
home he called his wife and said, 'Wife, put your
best dress on and those gold bracelets, all of them, and
give me my fur coat.' Hodja Effendi and his wife
returned to the wedding. From the entrance on he was
overwhelmed with compliments, was given the best seat
at the table, offered food, drinks, sweets. Smiling, he
began to dip the sleeve of his fur coat into the dishes saying,
'Help yourself, my fur coat. Go on, have a nibble of
domatesli pilav, a spoonful of Istanbul pilav,
some Iç pilav, help yourself.
'What are you doing Hodja Effendi?' cried the host.
'I was just inviting my fur coat to partake of these delicious
dishes since it seems to command so much respect!'
'How Effendi?'
'Why, an hour ago when I was here without my fur coat
I wasn't even noticed. Now I am
being overwhelmed with respect and attention.
So, help yourself, my fur coat!'*

TRABZON HAMSI TAVASI
Anchovy Rice
——— • • • ———

Trabzon (the ancient Trapezus) was one of the most remarkable cities of Asia Minor. It was a great centre of Greek culture and trade – the Romans conducted their trade with India via Trabzon.

Hamsi (anchovy) is found in abundance in this part of the Black Sea and it has created, over the generations, a certain myth about itself with folksongs and parables which endow this insignificant fish with quasi-religious powers. There is even a small village named after it. Once populated by Greeks, today the majority of the people in Trabzon are Lazes. This, in fact, is one of the few authentic Laz dishes found in Turkey.

700 g (1½ lb) fresh anchovies, cleaned and boned
60 ml (4 tablespoons) salt
75 g (3 oz) butter
350 g (12 oz) long grain rice, washed thoroughly under cold water and drained
1 onion, skinned and finely chopped
900 ml (1½ pints) water, boiling
45 ml (3 tablespoons) hazelnuts, halved *or* 45 ml (3 tablespoons) pine kernels *or* blanched, slivered almonds

10 ml (2 teaspoons) sugar
30 ml (2 tablespoons) sultanas
3.75 ml (¾ teaspoon) allspice
7.5 ml (1½ teaspoons) salt
3.75 ml (¾ teaspoon) cinnamon
2.5 ml (½ teaspoon) freshly ground black pepper
Garnish
2.5 ml (½ teaspoon) dillweed
5 ml (1 teaspoon) paprika
15 ml (1 tablespoon) *sumak*, optional (see Glossary)

Place the anchovies in a large pan, sprinkle with the salt and set aside.

Melt 50 g (2 oz) of the butter in a large saucepan, add the onion and fry for 5–10 minutes until soft. Add the rice and fry for a few minutes, stirring frequently. Stir in the water, nuts, sugar, sultanas, allspice, salt, cinnamon and black pepper and bring to the boil. Allow to boil vigorously for 3 minutes and then lower the heat, cover the pan and simmer for 15–20 minutes until the liquid has been absorbed.

Grease a large casserole dish, and heat the oven to 190°C (375°F) gas mark 5.

Rinse the anchovies thoroughly under cold water and then arrange half of them in a single layer in the dish. Tip the rice mixture into the dish and level it out. Arrange the remaining anchovies over the top.

Melt the remaining butter and pour it over the top. Cover the dish and cook in the oven for 15–20 minutes or until the fish are cooked.

Remove from the oven, sprinkle with the garnishes and serve with a salad.

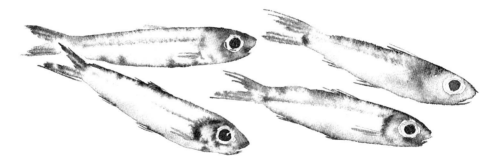

ALI PAŞA PILAVI
Meatballs and Nut Pilav
—— • • ——

Ali Paşa must have been a gourmet of great repute as there are many dishes in the Turkish cuisine bearing his name. If this recipe is typical of his taste then he was also an excellent artist. This is really a magnificent *pilav*, in appearance as well as flavour.

450 g (1 lb) minced meat
2.5 ml (½ teaspoon) salt
1.25 ml (¼ teaspoon) black pepper
1.25 ml (¼ teaspoon) chilli pepper
2 slices bread, crusts removed
30 ml (2 tablespoons) flour

60 ml (4 tablespoons) butter
1 quantity plain rice *pilav* – see *Pirinç Pilavi*
2 sheets *filo* pastry (see Glossary)
45 ml (3 tablespoons) pine kernels

Place the meat in a mixing bowl with the salt and peppers. Soak the bread in water, squeeze out excess water and crumble the bread into the bowl. Knead for several minutes until well blended and smooth. Dampen your palms and form the mixture into marble-sized balls. Roll the balls in the flour.

Heat 30 ml (2 tablespoons) of the butter in a pan, add some of the meatballs and fry for 8–10 minutes or until cooked through. Remove with a slotted spoon and cook the remaining meatballs in the same way. Set aside and keep warm.

Prepare the rice *pilav* following the instructions for *Pirinç Pilavi* (p. 27).

While the rice is cooking, heat the oven to 400°F (200°C) gas mark 6 and prepare the mould for the rice. To do this first melt 15 ml (1 tablespoon) of the remaining butter and use some of it to brush the bottom and sides of a round cake tin about 17.5 cm (7 inches) in diameter. Open out the sheets of *filo* pastry and brush the upper surface of each with some of the melted butter. Fold each sheet in half lengthways to form narrow strips. Arrange one of the strips around the inside edge of the cake tin and brush inside surface of the pastry with some of the butter. Arrange the second strip of pastry inside the first.

Tip the just-cooked rice into the cake tin and spread evenly. Trim off any pastry which is showing. Place the tin in the oven and cook for 10–15 minutes.

While this is cooking melt the remaining 15 ml (1 tablespoon) of butter in a small pan and fry the pine kernels until golden.

Remove the cake tin from the oven, place a large plate over the top and invert. The cake *pilav* should be golden on the top with golden flaky pastry sides.

Pile the meatballs on top of the cake, sprinkle with the pine kernels and serve.

IÇ PILAVI
Chicken Liver and Onion Pilav

'His liver is not worth tuppence.'
– A worthless person.

————— · • · —————

A fabulous rice dish often eaten on its own although it also goes well with roast meats and kebabs. I like to think of it as a Turkish *risotto* full of nuts and spices.

75 ml (5 tablespoons) butter
45 ml (3 tablespoons) pine kernels
45 ml (3 tablespoons) almonds
225 g (½ lb) chicken livers, cut into 1-cm (½-inch) pieces
1 onion, skinned and thinly sliced
2 tomatoes, blanched, peeled and chopped
1 medium head celery, finely sliced
7.5 ml (1½ teaspoons) salt
2.5 ml (½ teaspoon) freshly ground black pepper

15 ml (1 tablespoon) dried dillweed
15 ml (1 tablespoon) dried basil
350 g (12 oz) long grain rice, washed under cold water and drained
900 ml (1½ pints) meat or vegetable stock or water, boiling
45 ml (3 tablespoons) sultanas
45 ml (3 tablespoons) parsley, finely chopped

Melt 15 ml (1 tablespoon) of the butter in a small saucepan. Add the pine kernels and almonds and fry for a few minutes, until golden, stirring frequently. Remove with a slotted spoon and set aside.

Add another 15 ml (1 tablespoon) of butter to the pan and add the chicken livers, onion, tomatoes, celery, salt and pepper and fry for a few minutes until the onion is soft and the liver lightly browned. Add the dill and basil and return the nut mixture to the pan. Stir over a medium heat for a few more minutes and then remove the pan from the heat and set aside.

Melt the remaining butter in a large saucepan, add the rice and fry for 2–3 minutes, stirring frequently. Add the stock and sultanas and bring to the boil. Cover the pan, lower the heat and simmer for 15–20 minutes or until the liquid has been absorbed.

Fold the chicken liver mixture gently into the rice. Cover the rice with a tea towel, replace the lid and leave to 'rest' for 10–15 minutes. Fluff up gently with a long-pronged fork, add the parsley and serve.

MELEK PILAVI
Vermicelli Pilav

————— · • · —————

Ingredients as for *Pirinç Pilavi* (see p. 27) plus

50 g (2 oz) vermicelli, broken into 2.5-cm (1-inch) pieces

Fry the vermicelli in the melted butter until golden, stirring frequently. Add the rice and proceed as with the recipe for Pirinç Pilavi.

KARIDESLI PILAV
Rice with Prawns
———— • • • ————

The prawns from the Sea of Marmara are some of the largest and tastiest in the world. For thousands of years fishermen have gathered them in their small boats. The Turks, of course, were not a seafaring people and it fell to the lot of the Greeks in the Empire to be the fishermen.

This dish is a *risotto* of prawns, onion, tomatoes, rice and saffron. It is an attractive dish with a pinkish colour which is often eaten on its own with a salad and lemon wedges.

50 g (2 oz) butter
450 g (1 lb) prawns, fresh or frozen and thawed
1 onion, skinned and finely chopped
2 garlic cloves, skinned and crushed
3 tomatoes, blanched, peeled and chopped
3 sticks celery, thinly sliced
1.25 ml (¼ teaspoon) crushed saffron strands soaked in 30 ml (2 tablespoons) boiling water for 20 minutes

350 g (12 oz) long grain rice, washed under cold water and drained
900 ml (1½ pints) fish stock *or* water, boiling
5 ml (1 teaspoon) salt
2.5 ml (½ teaspoon) freshly ground black pepper
Garnish
lemon slices

Melt the butter in a large saucepan, add the prawns and fry for 2 minutes, stirring frequently. Remove with a slotted spoon and keep warm.

Add the onion and garlic to the pan and fry for about 5 minutes or until the onion is soft, but not brown. Add the tomatoes and celery and cook for a further 2–3 minutes. Add the saffron, rice, salt and pepper and stir well. Stir in the stock or water and bring back to the boil. Lower the heat and simmer until the liquid has been absorbed. Arrange the prawns on top of the rice, turn off the heat and leave to steam for 10–15 minutes. Stir gently with a long-pronged fork and turn into a large serving dish. Serve garnished with the lemon slices.

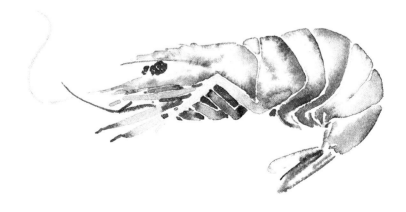

BULGUR PILAVI
Cracked Wheat Pilav
———— · ● · ————

Cracked wheat (burghul) is the basic cereal in Armenian cuisine and for the Anatolian villagers. The Turks are traditionally rice-eaters due to their ancestry from Central Asia where, even today, burghul is unheard of. This cereal was known to the Ancient Hittites, Urartians and Assyrians whose descendants, the few that are left, are still avid consumers of this wholesome grain.

This recipe is the standard one served throughout Turkey and Armenia. Burghul is used in much the same way as rice and so you can substitute the rice in any of the preceding recipes with burghul if you wish. If doing so reduce the 900 ml (1½ pints) of liquid suggested to 600 ml (1 pint).

50 g (2 oz) butter or *ghee*
1 onion, skinned and finely chopped
350 g (12 oz) large grain burghul

5 ml (1 teaspoon) salt
600 ml (1 pint) stock or water, boiling

Place the burghul in a fine sieve and wash with cold water until the water runs clear. Leave to drain.

Melt the butter in a large saucepan, add the onion and fry for 5 minutes until soft and golden. Add the burghul and fry for 2–3 minutes, stirring frequently. Stir in the salt and stock or water and bring to the boil. Boil vigorously for 3 minutes and then lower the heat and simmer, uncovered, for about 10 minutes until the liquid is absorbed.

Turn off the heat, cover the pan with a tea towel, fit on the lid and leave to 'rest' for 10–15 minutes. Fluff up gently with a long-pronged fork and serve.

PILIÇ BULGUR PILAVI
Burghul Pilav *with Poussins*
———— · ● · ————

Traditionally, small chicken or poussin are used in this recipe, but you can substitute half a chicken if you wish.

This really is a meal in its own right when served with yogurt and/or a fresh salad, but it is sometimes served as part of a larger meal with kebabs or roasts.

2 poussins or ½ chicken
350 g (12 oz) large grain burghul
50 g (2 oz) butter or *ghee*
1 onion, skinned and finely chopped
25 g (1 oz) vermicelli, broken into
  2.5-cm (1-inch) pieces
3 green chilli peppers, seeded and thinly
  sliced

600 ml (1 pint) chicken stock
30 ml (2 tablespoons) sultanas
5 ml (1 teaspoon) salt
2.5 ml (½ teaspoon) allspice
2 cloves

Place the poussins or chicken in a large saucepan, cover with water and bring to the boil. Lower the heat and simmer for 30–45 minutes or until tender. Remove the poussins and set aside to cool. Reserve the stock.

Place the burghul in a fine sieve and wash under cold water until the water runs clear. Leave to drain.

When the poussins are cool enough to handle cut each one into 8 pieces – 2 breasts, 2 wings, 2 drumsticks and 2 thighs. Remove the skin. If using half a chicken, discard the skin and bones and cut the flesh into bite-sized pieces.

Melt the butter in a large saucepan, add the chicken pieces and fry for 5–10 minutes until evenly golden. Remove with a slotted spoon and reserve. Add the onion, vermicelli and chilli peppers to the pan and fry for about 5 minutes until the onion is soft and the vermicelli golden. Add the burghul and fry for 1–2 minutes, stirring frequently. Return the chicken pieces to the pan and stir in all the remaining ingredients. Bring to the boil. Lower the heat and simmer until the liquid is absorbed.

Turn off heat, cover with a tea towel and lid and leave to 'rest' for 10–15 minutes. Turn into a large serving dish and serve.

KABAK DANDERMA
Pumpkin with Rice

*'The mouse could not squeeze through the
hole and besides, he had a pumpkin tied to his tail.'*
– Complications to an already difficult situation.

––––––– • • • –––––––

This is a speciality of the city of Karput and makes exciting use of pumpkin with rice. It is a particular favourite of Armenians and can be served with meat, fish or poultry – particularly roasts and kebabs.

This dish has a fascinating, slightly sweet flavour.

250 g (9 oz) long grain rice, washed thoroughly under cold water and drained	450 g (1 lb) pumpkin, peeled and with flesh cut lengthways into 1-cm (½-inch) thick slices
7.5 ml (1½ teaspoons) salt	75 g (3 oz) sugar
75 g (3 oz) sultanas	110 g (4 oz) butter, melted

Put the rice into a large saucepan, add 1.2 litres (2 pints) hot water and bring quickly to the boil. Simmer for 10 minutes. Add the salt and sultanas, mix thoroughly and simmer for a further 5 minutes. Remove from the heat, strain into a sieve and run cold water through the rice.

Generously grease a large baking dish or casserole. Arrange half the pumpkin slices over the bottom of the dish. Sprinkle 25 g (1 oz) of the sugar and 25 g (1 oz) of the melted butter over the pumpkin.

In a large bowl mix together 25 g (1 oz) of the remaining sugar and 25 g (1 oz) of the remaining melted butter. Add the rice and mix thoroughly. Arrange the rice evenly over the pumpkin slices and set aside.

Meanwhile pour the remaining melted butter into a large frying pan and fry the remaining pumpkin slices, turning several times so that they are well coated with the butter. Remove with a slotted spoon and arrange decoratively over the rice. Sprinkle with the remaining sugar.

CHAPTER THREE

SALATALAR VE SEBZELER
Salads and Vegetables

'He who mixes with the vegetable seller smells of his perfume.'

Vegetables are usually eaten raw with a sprinkling of salt. In Turkey, as with neighbouring Iran and the Caucasus, much use is made of fresh herbs such as coriander, parsley, basil, marjoram, dill and tarragon. These herbs are not only chopped and added to raw and cooked salads, but are often eaten rolled up in thin pieces of bread and consumed like sandwiches.

The three basic dressing ingredients for most salads are lemon juice, olive oil and yogurt. Vinegar and mayonnaise are only popular along the western coast of the country.

Olive oil forms the basis of all cold vegetable dishes, while butter is used for the warm dishes. In the past, and even today in Anatolia, the fat from the tail end of a sheep (*küyruk yaği*) replaces both olive oil and butter. This rendered-down fat has a marvellous flavour and aroma and although it tends to be rather heavy no substitute will do it justice. So naturally the warm recipes in this book will not taste quite the same as they do when cooked in a peasant kitchen in the heartland of Anatolia.

Yogurt, fresh from goat, sheep or cow's milk, is perhaps the most popular ingredient available. It is mixed with garlic and poured over *pilavs* and stews and, of course, is incorporated into many salads. By far the most well known and most loved is *çaçik*, which is a yogurt and cucumber salad. When there is nothing left to eat the villager turns to this salad in desperation and, no doubt, with relish as the few lines from Mahmut Makal's vivid description of his village life shows: *'Spring came and relishes ran out. Even flour was scarce – now everyone ate* çaçik pilav *in the morning,* çaçik pilav *at mid-day and* çaçik pilav *again in the evening. Those of use who had no flour had* çaçik *alone – when I say* çaçik *don't think I mean an appetising salad, eaten with yogurt. Here,* çaçik *means edible weeds.'*

BIZIM KOY

I have included 3 traditional recipes for *çaçik*. The first is the standard one popular throughout the Middle East and the others are regional specialities.

ÇAÇIKI
Yogurt and Cucumber Salad
——— • ● • ———

You can serve this salad with almost everything – roasts, stews, kebabs, *pilavs*, stuffed vegetables and it is frequently part of the *meze* table.

600 ml (1 pint) yogurt
2.5 ml (½ teaspoon) salt
1 garlic clove, skinned and crushed
1 cucumber, peeled, quartered
lengthways and finely chopped

30 ml (2 tablespoons) finely chopped
fresh mint *or* 10 ml (2 teaspoons)
dried mint
Garnish
pinch cayenne pepper

Place the yogurt in a mixing bowl and stir in all the remaining ingredients. Chill until ready to serve.

Pour into either a serving dish or individual bowls and garnish with a little cayenne pepper.

BINGÖL ÇAÇIKI
Thousand Lakes Çaçik

'Look at the mint he's eating.'
– What a silly thing to say!
——— • ● • ———

From the small town of Bingöl high up in the mountains of Eastern Turkey comes this lovely salad. The raisins and pomegranate seeds represent the thousand lakes after which the town is named.

600 ml (1 pint) yogurt
2.5 ml (½ teaspoon) salt
1 garlic clove, skinned and crushed
2 carrots, peeled and grated
30 ml (2 tablespoons) raisins

30 ml (2 tablespoons) finely chopped
fresh mint *or* 10 ml (2 teaspoons)
dried mint
seeds 1 pomegranate

Place the yogurt in a bowl and add all the remaining ingredients except for a few of the pomegranate seeds. Chill until ready to serve.

Serve in individual bowls with a few pomegranate seeds sprinkled over the top of each.

BIBERLI ÇAÇIKI
Yogurt and Pepper Salad
—— • ● • ——

This hot pepper version of the yogurt salad is a speciality of the city of Manisa which is the ancient Greek city of Magnesia ad Sipylum. Incidentally, it is reputed to have been founded by the legendary Amazons. During the Byzantine period it was one of the greatest cities in western Anatolia.

6 small, green, hot chillies
600 ml (1 pint) yogurt
5 ml (1 teaspoon) salt
1 garlic clove, skinned and crushed

45 ml (3 tablespoons) parsley, finely
   chopped
30 ml (2 tablespoons) olive oil

Grill the peppers for 4–5 minutes, turning once. When cool enough to handle peel off the skins and remove and discard the seeds. Cut the peppers into small pieces about ½ cm (¼ inch) square.

Pour the yogurt into a large bowl, add the salt and garlic and stir thoroughly. Mix in the peppers and parsley.

Serve in small individual bowls with a little olive oil poured over each.

SALATALIK
Cucumber Salad
—— • ● • ——

This is a simple salad of cucumber, olives and cheese which is popular with the peasants who eat it with home-baked hot bread. It makes a fine hors d'oeuvre or supper dish and it can be served as an accompaniment to kebab dishes.

1 cucumber, peeled and thinly sliced
50 g (2 oz) black olives, stoned and
   thinly sliced
110 g (4 oz) feta cheese or other crumbly
   white cheese

Dressing
30 ml (2 tablespoons) lemon juice
15 ml (1 tablespoon) olive oil
2.5 ml (½ teaspoon) salt
15 ml (1 tablespoon) dried mint

Place the cucumber and olive slices in a salad bowl. Mix the dressing ingredients together, pour over the salad and toss thoroughly.

Crumble the cheese, sprinkle it over the salad and serve.

HAVUÇ SALATASI
Carrot Salad
—— • ● • ——

A warm salad of fried carrots with yogurt – typically Anatolian. Serve with any meat dish.

700 g (1½ lb) carrots, peeled and cut into
   ½-cm (¼-inch) thick rings
5 ml (1 teaspoon) salt
30 ml (2 tablespoons) seasoned flour
oil

300 ml (½ pint) yogurt
Garnish
2.5 ml (½ teaspoon) freshly ground
   black pepper
2.5 ml (½ teaspoon) cinnamon

Place the carrots in a saucepan, cover with water and add the salt. Bring to the boil and simmer until just tender. Drain and pat dry with kitchen paper.

Place the seasoned flour in a bowl, add the carrot slices and toss until well coated.

Heat a little oil in a frying pan, add some carrot slices and fry until golden, turning once. Remove with a slotted spoon and keep warm while you fry the remaining slices in the same way. Add more oil if necessary.

Meanwhile warm the yogurt gently, but do not let it boil.

Turn the carrots into a serving dish, pour the warmed yogurt evenly over them and sprinkle with the black pepper and cinnamon. Serve immediately.

PORTAKAL SALATASI

Orange and Onion Salad

*'Don't offer diamonds to men who deal
in onions.'*

———— • ● • ————

A most unusual combination of oranges, onions and black olives which makes a marvellous salad. It is typically Middle Eastern and particularly Turkish. Excellent with all roasts.

4 oranges, peeled and with white pith discarded	15 ml (1 tablespoon) lemon juice
2 onions, skinned and thinly sliced	*Garnish*
100 g (4 oz) black olives	lettuce leaves
60 ml (4 tablespoons) olive oil	pinch paprika
	pinch cumin

Cut the oranges into rounds about ½ cm (¼ inch) thick.

Line a large serving plate with the lettuce leaves and then arrange the orange and onion slices decoratively over them. Sprinkle the olives over the top.

Mix the oil and lemon juice together and pour over the salad. Sprinkle with the paprika and cumin and serve.

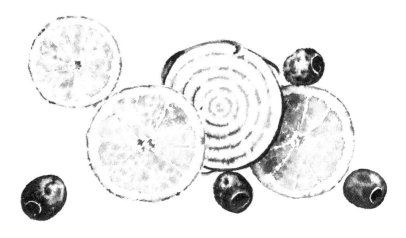

ÇOBAN SALATASI
Shepherd's Salad
— • • • —

A most popular salad from the mountains of Anatolia.
This is a traditional accompaniment for any roast or kebab.

4 tomatoes, thinly sliced
1 medium cucumber, peeled and thinly
  sliced
1 small onion, skinned and thinly sliced
1 small red pepper, thinly sliced
1 small green pepper, thinly sliced
2–3 spring onions, thinly sliced
1 Cos lettuce, washed and patted dry
  with kitchen paper

Dressing
45 ml (3 tablespoons) olive oil

30 ml (2 tablespoons) lemon juice
10 ml (2 teaspoons) dried mint
2.5 ml (½ teaspoon) chilli pepper
5 ml (1 teaspoon) salt
2.5 ml (½ teaspoon) freshly ground
  black pepper

Garnish
30 ml (2 tablespoons) parsley, finely
  chopped
3–4 radishes, thinly sliced

Place the sliced vegetables in a large salad bowl. Shred the lettuce leaves and add to the bowl.

Mix all the dressing ingredients thoroughly and pour over the vegetables. Toss the salad well, sprinkle with the garnishes and serve.

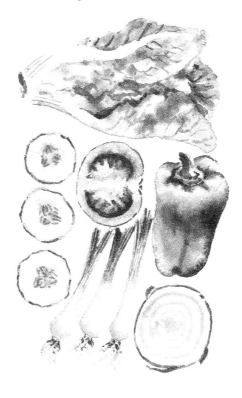

TAVALAR
To Fry
—— • • • ——

Tava (from the Arabic *tawah*) is the Turkish name for a frying pan and much is made of this simple kitchen utensil. Vegetables, fish and meat are fried in many a wondrous way.

Vegetables are never boiled, unless for medicinal purposes, but are always fried in butter or oil first whether they are to be used for salads, soups or stews.

The most popular vegetables for frying are courgettes, aubergines, mushrooms, artichokes and French beans. Fried vegetables are served as an accompaniment to roasts, as an entree with yogurt poured over the top or as fillings for a sandwich. These vegetables can be eaten cold, on a *meze* table, or warm. They are very tasty and are simple to prepare.

KABAK MUJVERI
Courgette and Meat Rissoles

'She opens up like a marrow flower.'
– She is too forward.
—— • • • ——

I had often wondered what Middle Eastern housewives did with the flesh of the courgettes and aubergines which is scooped out when *dolma* (p. 18) is being prepared. The answer is simple. It is not discarded as I had supposed, but is mixed with meat to make this dish or a meatless version with eggs and mint. Eat with a rice *pilav* and/or fresh salad.

8 medium courgettes, peeled	5 ml (1 teaspoon) salt
450 g (1 lb) minced meat	2.5 ml (½ teaspoon) freshly ground
2 eggs	black pepper
1 onion, skinned and very finely	5 ml (1 teaspoon) cumin
chopped	2.5 ml (½ teaspoon) paprika
50 g (2 oz) grated cheese e.g. feta or any	*To Fry*
crumbly white cheese	flour
30 ml (2 tablespoons) flour	oil
45 ml (3 tablespoons) parsley *or* dill,	*Garnish*
finely chopped	lettuce leaves

Put the courgette flesh in a large bowl. If you are using the courgettes for *dolma* then much of the flesh will be saved, but you will have to grate any large pieces. Otherwise peel the courgettes and grate the flesh.

Add all the remaining ingredients and knead until well blended and smooth.

Dampen your hands, take a tablespoon of the mixture and shape between your palms to form a round, flat rissole. Repeat until all the mixture is used.

Heat some oil in a frying pan. Coat each rissole with flour, place 3 or 4 in the pan and fry gently for 10–15 minutes, turning once, until cooked through and golden. Remove and keep warm while you cook the remaining rissoles in the same way.

Serve on a bed of lettuce leaves.

YOĞURTLU PATLICAN
Fried Aubergines with Yogurt
———— • ● • ————

This is one of over 200 aubergine recipes of which Turkish cuisine boasts. It is a simple recipe for fried aubergine slices topped with spiced yogurt. Other vegetables, such as cauliflower, mushrooms, carrots or beans can be prepared in the same way. Serve either as an hors d'oeuvre with pita bread or accompanying all kinds of roast meats and kebabs.

3 aubergines, wiped clean and cut into
½-cm (¼-inch) thick rings
30 ml (2 tablespoons) salt
150 ml–300 ml (¼–½ pint) olive oil or
vegetable oil
300 ml (½ pint) yogurt

2 garlic cloves, skinned and crushed
2.5 ml (½ teaspoon) caraway seeds
1.25 ml (¼ teaspoon) salt
Garnish
few sprigs fresh dill
pinch paprika

Arrange the aubergine slices over a large plate, sprinkle with the salt, top with another plate and set aside for 30 minutes. Rinse the slices thoroughly and pat dry with kitchen paper.

Heat some of the oil in a frying pan, add a few of the slices and fry until soft and golden, turning once. Remove with a slotted spoon and keep warm while you fry the remaining slices in the same way. Add more oil when necessary.

Meanwhile place the yogurt, garlic, caraway seeds and salt in a bowl and mix thoroughly.

Arrange the aubergine slices on a serving plate, pour the spiced yogurt over them and garnish with the dill sprigs and paprika.

BAHÇE GÜZELI
Pretty Garden

'His mother an onion, his father garlic, himself comes out conserve of rose.'
———— • ● • ————

This delicious dish of peas and shallots makes a good accompaniment to meat and poultry roasts and grills.

450 g (1 lb) peas
about 20 shallots, skinned and left whole
5 ml (1 teaspoon) salt
5 ml (1 teaspoon) sugar

600 ml (1 pint) vegetable or meat stock
15 ml (1 tablespoon) oil
30 ml (2 tablespoons) sifted flour

Place the peas in a saucepan with the shallots, salt, sugar and stock. Cover the pan and simmer over a low heat for 20 minutes.

In a small bowl mix the oil and flour together.

Hold a fine sieve over the pan and pour the oil-flour mixture into it. Rub the mixture through on to the peas and stir carefully. Cover the pan and simmer for a further 5 minutes. Serve immediately.

PRASA YAHNISI
Stewed Leeks
— • • —

An easy to prepare and tasty vegetable dish which is excellent with all meat dishes. It is equally successful hot or cold. Kurds and Armenians often eat it accompanied by yogurt or soured cream.

900 g (2 lb) leeks	2.5 ml (½ teaspoon) freshly ground
150 ml (¼ pint) olive oil	black pepper
2 onions, skinned and sliced into rings	1.25 ml (¼ teaspoon) cayenne pepper
2 large tomatoes, blanched, peeled and	*Garnish*
chopped	30 ml (2 tablespoons) parsley, finely
5 ml (1 teaspoon) salt	chopped

Cut the roots and most of the green tops off the leeks and remove any coarse outer leaves. Cut each leek in half lengthways and then cut into 2.5-cm (1-inch) pieces. Place in a colander and wash very thoroughly under cold, running water.

Heat the olive oil in a large saucepan, add the onion rings and fry for 5 minutes, stirring frequently, until soft. Add the leeks and turn several times to coat with the oil. Add the remaining ingredients and stir well. Cover the pan and cook over a low heat for about 30 minutes, stirring occasionally.

Transfer to a large dish, sprinkle with the parsley and serve hot or cold.

MIDYE TAVASI
Fried Mussels
— • • —

The mussels are dipped in a batter of beer and egg yolks, deep-fried until golden and then served with *Tarator* Sauce (p. 94). This speciality of Istanbul is delicious with a fresh salad.

About 40 mussels. Make sure that when	300 ml (½ pint) beer
you buy them they are tightly closed –	2 egg yolks
this is a sign of freshness. Discard any	2.5 ml (½ teaspoon) bicarbonate of soda
that are not.	5 ml (1 teaspoon) salt
Batter	*To Cook*
50 g (2 oz) cornflour	oil for deep-frying
50 g (2 oz) plain flour	

Scrub the mussels and immerse in water. Take one at a time from the water and force it open with a sharp knife. Scoop out the flesh, trim off the black part and the beard and drop each mussel into a bowl of cold water.

Prepare the batter by mixing all the ingredients together thoroughly in a bowl to form a paste thick enough to coat the back of a spoon.

Heat enough oil in a pan to deep-fry. Dip each mussel into the batter and then into the oil. Fry for 3–4 minutes or until golden. Remove with a slotted spoon and keep warm while you cook the remaining mussels.

KABAK TAVASI
Fried Courgettes
———— · • · ————

450 g (1 lb) courgettes or baby marrows, washed and topped and tailed
30 ml (2 tablespoons) salt
150 ml–300 ml (¼–½ pint) olive oil or cooking oil
2 garlic cloves, skinned and crushed
30–45 ml (2–3 tablespoons) lemon juice or vinegar

Cut the courgettes into ½-cm (¼-inch) thick rings and spread out on a large plate. Sprinkle with the salt and set aside for 20–30 minutes. Rinse and pat dry with kitchen paper.

Heat some of the oil in a frying pan, add the garlic and fry for 1–2 minutes. Add some of the courgette slices and fry until tender and golden on both sides. Remove with a slotted spoon and keep warm while you cook the remaining slices in the same way. Add more oil if necessary.

Pour a little lemon juice or vinegar over them and serve.

FASULYE ZEYTIN YAĞLI
Green Beans in Oil

'A bean will not get wet in his mouth.' – A chatterbox.
———— · • · ————

One of the most popular olive oil-based vegetable dishes, this is a special favourite of the Anatolians. Like many olive oil-based dishes this can be eaten hot or cold, although I prefer it cold.

700 g (1½ lb) French beans
120 ml (8 tablespoons) olive oil
1 large onion, skinned and thinly sliced
6 tomatoes, blanched, peeled and quartered
3 garlic cloves, skinned and crushed
5 ml (1 teaspoon) salt
2.5 ml (½ teaspoon) freshly ground black pepper
2.5 ml (½ teaspoon) allspice
water
30 ml (2 tablespoons) lemon juice

Wash, top and tail the beans and then snap each one in half.

Heat the oil in a large saucepan, add the onion and fry for 5–10 minutes until soft, stirring frequently.

Add the tomatoes and fry for a further 2–3 minutes. Mix in the beans, garlic, salt, pepper and allspice.

Add enough water to cover the vegetables and stir well. Bring to the boil, lower the heat and simmer for about 1 hour or until the beans are tender. Remove from the heat and leave to cool.

When cold stir in the lemon juice and turn into a serving dish.

CHAPTER FOUR

FIRIN KEBABLARI
Oven Kebabs and Stews

'Bunu yapman için kirk firin ekmek yemen hazim.'

– You would have to eat all the bread in the bakery to be capable of doing that. (Said to boastful people.)

F*irin* kebabs are stews of vegetables on their own or with meat. This type of cooking is of very ancient origins going back to the beginnings of our civilisation. Before man had settled down and built himself a shelter and a *firin* (oven), the family's fare was cooked in a *kazan* (cauldron). The nomads' entire meal often comprised the contents of a cauldron and therefore the food was both limited in ingredients and heavy for digestion.

The nomadic origin of the Turkish people is well reflected in the numerous so-called *firin kebablari* which, in reality, were meals cooked in large cauldrons. The name kebab here is a misnomer as it usually applies to meat cuts cooked on a wood or charcoal fire and not in a saucepan or in the oven. These are very simple, economical and tasty dishes and should be served with a rice or burghul *pilav* of your choice.

The first recipe is a classic, equally popular with Armenians and Kurds. The recipe is a family one given to me by my mother who, no doubt, received it from hers – this is what tradition is about, and one cannot get more traditional than this marvellously succulent dish from Anatolia.

KAZAN KEBABI
Pot Kebab
—— • ● • ——

6 medium aubergines
6 large tomatoes
water
5 ml (1 teaspoon) salt
5 ml (1 teaspoon) dillweed
Filling
450 g (1 lb) minced lamb or beef
1 large green pepper, seeded and
   chopped
1 onion, skinned and finely chopped

4 large tomatoes, blanched, peeled and
   chopped
45 ml (3 tablespoons) parsley, finely
   chopped
30 ml (2 tablespoons) tomato purée
7.5 ml (1½ teaspoons) salt
2.5 ml (½ teaspoon) freshly ground
   black pepper
2.5 ml (½ teaspoon) chilli pepper

Preheat the oven to 200°C (400°F) gas mark 6. Place all the filling ingredients in a large bowl and then knead until the mixture is well blended and smooth.

With a sharp knife peel strips of skin lengthways off each aubergine to give them an attractive stripy appearance. Slice the aubergines, at 1-cm (½-inch) intervals, crossways about ¾ of the way through so that all the slices remain attached at the bottom. Cut down through the tomatoes in the same way.

Remove a spoonful of the meat mixture and roll into a ball. Press gently between your palms to form a rissole. Repeat until all the meat has been made into small rissoles.

Place a rissole in each gap in each tomato and aubergine.

Arrange the vegetables tightly in an ovenproof dish so that they keep their shape and hold the meat in place. Add enough water to half cover the vegetables and sprinkle with the salt and dillweed.

Cook in the oven for about 1 hour or until the meat and vegetables are well cooked. Remove from the oven and serve immediately straight from the dish.

MALATYA KEBABI
Oven-Baked Stuffed Aubergines
—— • ● • ——

This dish of aubergines stuffed with meat and onions and topped with tomatoes and green peppers comes from Malatya and is one of the classic dishes of the Ottoman Turkish cuisine. I emphasise the Ottoman origin since this dish, like many others from Turkey, is equally popular with Armenians, Kurds and Arabs. Serve with a rice or burghul *pilav*.

6 medium aubergines
120 ml (8 tablespoons) oil
1 large onion, skinned and finely
   chopped
450 g (1 lb) minced lamb or beef
5 ml (1 teaspoon) salt
2.5 ml (½ teaspoon) freshly ground
   black pepper

2.5 ml (½ teaspoon) paprika
3 tomatoes, blanched, peeled and
   chopped
300 ml (½ pint) water
3 tomatoes, quartered
3 green peppers, seeded and quartered

Cut the heads off the aubergines and then cut each vegetable in half lengthways. Remove some of the pulp from each half leaving shells about ½ cm (¼ inch) thick. Arrange the shells on a plate, sprinkle with 10 ml (2 teaspoons) of salt and set aside for 30 minutes.

Preheat the oven to 190°C (375°F) gas mark 5.

Rinse the aubergines under cold running water and pat dry with kitchen paper.

Heat 90 ml (6 tablespoons) of the oil in a frying pan, add the aubergine halves, a few at a time, and fry for about 3 minutes, turning regularly. Using a slotted spoon transfer the halves to a large, shallow casserole and arrange side by side.

Heat the remaining oil in a saucepan, add the onion and fry for 5–10 minutes until soft, stirring occasionally. Stir in the meat, salt, pepper, paprika and chopped tomatoes and fry for a further 5 minutes. Add the water and cook for 30 minutes, stirring regularly to prevent the meat sticking to the pan.

Remove from the heat and fill each aubergine half with some of the meat mixture. Place a tomato and green pepper quarter on top of each aubergine half and pour any remaining pan juices into the casserole.

Bake in the oven for about 30 minutes. Remove from the oven and serve.

PAPAZ KEBABI
The Priest's Kebab
—— • ● • ——

This is a very ancient dish from Eastern Turkey where milk is added to the meat – contrary to Semitic and hence Muslim custom, where milk and meat are not permitted to be consumed together.

Traditionally a rice *pilav* accompanies this kebab, but nowadays potatoes and other vegetables are often served.

45 ml (3 tablespoons) butter	5 ml (1 teaspoon) salt
2 onions, skinned and thinly sliced	15 ml (1 tablespoon) plain flour
700 g (1½ lb) lean lamb or beef, cut into	450 ml (¾ pint) milk
6 pieces	2.5 ml (½ teaspoon) salt
600 ml (1 pint) water	

Melt 30 ml (2 tablespoons) of the butter in a large saucepan. Add the onions and fry for 5–10 minutes, stirring frequently, until soft. Add the pieces of meat, cover the saucepan and cook for 10 minutes. After 5 minutes uncover the pan and stir the meat mixture before covering again.

Meanwhile preheat the oven to 180°C (350°F) gas mark 4.

After the 10 minutes uncover the pan, add the water and salt, stir and continue simmering until the water has evaporated. Remove from the heat and keep warm.

Melt the remaining butter in a small pan, remove from the heat and stir in the flour. Gradually add the milk, stirring constantly, until the mixture is smooth. Season with the salt, return to a low heat and cook, stirring constantly, until the mixture thickens.

Transfer the meat and onion mixture to an ovenproof casserole and pour the white sauce over the top. Cook in the oven for 20 minutes and serve.

THE POT AND ITS OFFSPRING

One day the Hodja borrowed a large pot from
his neighbour Ali Effendi. The next day he
returned it with a smaller pot inside.
'My dear neighbour,' he said, 'I forgot to tell you.
Your pot gave birth to that small one while it was with us!'
Ali Effendi was amazed, but very gladly accepted both
the explanation and the small pot. A few days later
the Hodja again asked for the same large pot from his
neighbour who lent it to him with the greatest pleasure.
A week passed by and no news from the Hodja. After
a few more days Ali Effendi went to the Hodja's house.
'Hodja Effendi, what has happened to that
large pot I lent you?' he asked.
'Why, didn't you hear the sad news? Your pot died
two days after I borrowed it from you!'
'Come now Hodja Effendi, you don't expect me to believe
that. You know I know that a pot cannot die.'
'Well, you are a funny one!' replied the Hodja.
'You were quite happy to believe me when I said it had
given birth to a baby pot, but now that I say it has died
you have the affrontery to accuse me of lying.
How dare you ... get out!'

ETLI TAVŞAN GÜVEÇ KEBABI
Rabbit and Vegetable Stew

'*Tavsan boku ne kokor ne bulasir.*'
– Like a hare's droppings,
he is neither smelly nor messy.
(Said about an ineffectual person.)

———— · • · ————

This is a speciality from the town of Bolu, north-west Turkey, which was once part of Alexander's empire and was known as Claudiopolis. Both the towns of Bolu and Bursa, in the same region, are remarkable in having given birth to some of the best and most renowned chefs of the Turkish cuisine.

The rabbit is marinated overnight and then cooked with tomatoes and peppers. Serve with new potatoes or a *pilav*.

1–1.5 kg (2–3 lb) rabbit or hare, cut into 5-cm (2-inch) pieces
30 ml (2 tablespoons) butter
2 garlic cloves, skinned and crushed
2 bay leaves
4 large tomatoes, blanched, peeled and chopped
4 green peppers, seeded and cut into 2.5-cm (1-inch) pieces
1 green chilli pepper, seeded and thinly sliced
6–8 whole *sumak* seeds *or* 2.5 ml (½ teaspoon) *sumak* powder

Marinade
300 ml (½ pint) oil

300 ml (½ pint) dry white wine
1 small onion, skinned and finely chopped
2 bay leaves
2–3 cloves
10 whole black peppercorns
10 or more juniper berries (optional)
5 ml (1 teaspoon) thyme

To Serve
900 g (2 lb) new potatoes, scraped and halved
30 ml (2 tablespoons) butter, melted
5 ml (1 teaspoon) salt

Mix all the marinate ingredients together in a large bowl. Add the rabbit pieces, mix well, cover and leave to marinate for several hours or overnight. Stir occasionally.

Melt 30 ml (2 tablespoons) of the butter in a large saucepan. Remove the rabbit pieces from the marinade with a slotted spoon and transfer to the saucepan. Add the garlic, bay leaves, tomatoes, green peppers, chilli pepper and *sumak*. Stir well.

Cover the pan with a piece of greaseproof paper or a tea towel and then fit on the lid. If using a tea towel make sure you lift the edges on to the lid to prevent them catching fire. Reduce the heat to low and leave to steam for about 1½ hours.

Meanwhile drop the prepared potatoes into a pan of boiling water and cook for 1 minute. Drain. Arrange the potatoes in a large, greased tray and sprinkle with the melted butter and salt. Bake in an oven heated to 180°C (350°F) gas mark 4 for 20–30 minutes.

Serve the potatoes with the rabbit stew.

KÂĞIT KEBABI
Lamb in Foil Kebab

*'When the muttons are being sheared, the
young lambs tremble in fear.'*

— • • —

Meat baked in this way is very soft and tender. This dish is extremely delicious. Serve with
a rice *pilav* and a fresh salad.

75 g (3 oz) butter
900 g (2 lb) leg of lamb, cut into 6 pieces
1 large onion, skinned and chopped
2 large carrots, peeled and diced
3 tomatoes, blanched, peeled and
  chopped
5 ml (1 teaspoon) salt
5 ml (1 teaspoon) white pepper

2.5 ml (½ teaspoon) allspice
15 ml (1 tablespoon) chopped fresh dill
  or 5 ml (1 teaspoon) dried dillweed
3 potatoes, peeled and cut into thin
  rounds
75 g (3 oz) cooked peas
45 ml (3 tablespoons) chopped parsley

Melt the butter in a large saucepan, add the pieces of meat and fry for 5–10
minutes, turning occasionally, until evenly browned. Remove the pieces of meat
with a slotted spoon and reserve.

Add the onion, carrots, tomatoes, salt, pepper and dill to the pan, mix well and
cook over a low heat for about 20 minutes. Return the meat pieces to the pan,
cover and cook for about 1 hour. Meanwhile preheat the oven to 180°C (350°F)
gas mark 4.

Remove the meat and carrots with a slotted spoon and reserve in a warm place.

Add the sliced potatoes to the pan and simmer in the juices for 5 minutes.
Remove the slices and add to the meat and carrots, together with the cooked peas
and parsley.

Cut some silver foil into 6 22.5-cm (9-inch) squares.

Place 1 piece of meat, some of the vegetables and a little of the pan juices in the
centre of each square of foil and then bring the edges together and completely
seal each 'parcel'.

Place the parcels side by side in a baking dish, add a little water and bake in the
oven for 30–45 minutes. Serve immediately.

KONYA KEBABI
Steamed Lamb Kebab

— • • —

A speciality of the ancient capital of the Seljuks. Konya is one the oldest cities in the world
– at least 10,000 years old. Hittites, Romans and Greeks settled there, followed by Arabs
and the Seljuks. It was Kilic Arslan I (1097) who made it his capital city.

Konya, of course, is also famous for its Whirling Dervishes – once a ravishingly
beautiful, mystical and hypnotic sect who whirled round and round abandoning themselves to God's love, thus freeing themselves from earthly bondage.

900 g (2 lb) lean lamb, leg or shoulder
2 large onions, skinned and either quartered or cut into smaller pieces
3 tomatoes, blanched, peeled and sliced
3 medium aubergines, cut lengthways into 1-cm (½-inch) thick slices

2 green peppers, seeded and quartered
a few mint leaves *or* 5 ml (1 teaspoon) dried mint
7.5 ml (1½ teaspoons) salt
90 ml (6 tablespoons) water

Cut the meat into 7.5-cm (3-inch) pieces and put into an ovenproof casserole with a well-fitting lid. Place the vegetables and mint over the meat, sprinkle with the salt and add the water. Cover with the lid, sealing it as well as possible to prevent evaporation.

Place in an oven at 180°C (350°F) gas mark 4 and cook for 1½ hours.

Lower the heat to 160°C (300°F) gas mark 2 and cook for a further hour.

Remove from the oven and spoon into a serving dish. Accompany with a rice or burghul *pilav* and a salad.

BAHCEVAN KEBABI
Gardener's Kebab
———— • ● • ————

All the vegetables of the garden are found in this kebab which is in fact a rich stew usually served with bread or a rice *pilav*. The vegetables will vary according to the season and you can use chicken instead of lamb.

900 g (2 lb) lean lamb, cut into 5-cm (2-inch) pieces
5 ml (1 teaspoon) salt
2.5 ml (½ teaspoon) freshly ground black pepper
50 g (2 oz) butter
2 carrots, peeled and cut into 1-cm (½-inch) thick rings
2 turnips, peeled and cut into large chunks
450 ml (¾ pint) stock or water

3 tomatoes, blanched, peeled and quartered
450 g (1 lb) button onions
2 green peppers, seeded and coarsely chopped
30 ml (2 tablespoons) chopped fresh dill *or* 10 ml (2 teaspoons) dried dillweed
To Serve
yogurt
30 ml (2 tablespoons) chopped fresh mint or 10 ml (2 teaspoons) dried mint

Rub the salt and pepper into the pieces of meat.

Melt the butter in a large saucepan or casserole, add the meat pieces and fry, turning frequently, for about 15 minutes.

Add the carrots, turnips and stock or water and bring to the boil. Cover, lower the heat and simmer for 20–30 minutes.

Uncover, add the remaining ingredients, mix thoroughly, cover and continue cooking until all the vegetables and the meat are tender.

Remove from the heat, adjust seasoning if necessary and transfer to a large serving dish. Top each serving with a little yogurt and sprinkle with some mint.

KUZU ANKARA TAVASI
Ankara-Style Lamb Casserole

*'A person who has burnt his mouth will even
blow on a yogurt dish before he eats it.'*
– Anyone who has had trouble will always be
cautious afterwards.

• • •

This is a rich, creamy casserole which has a crust of lightly cooked egg over the surface. It is a delicious and colourful dish.

15 ml (1 tablespoon) butter
900 g (2 lb) lamb, leg or shoulder, cut into 6 equal pieces
1.2 litres (2 pints) water
5 ml (1 teaspoon) salt
2 onions, skinned and thinly sliced
1 large carrot, peeled and cut into ½-cm (¼-inch) thick rounds

100 g (4 oz) green beans.
450 ml (¾ pint) yogurt
50 g (2 oz) plain flour
2 eggs, lightly beaten
Garnish
15 ml (1 tablespoon) paprika
15 ml (1 tablespoon) dried dillweed

Melt the butter in a large saucepan, add the meat pieces and fry for a few minutes, turning occasionally, until evenly browned. Add the water and salt and bring quickly to the boil. Cover the pan, lower the heat and simmer for 45 minutes.

Add the onions and carrot and cook, uncovered, for 30 minutes.

Add the beans and cook for a further 5–10 minutes or until the beans are just tender.

Meanwhile preheat the oven to 190°C (375°F) gas mark 5.

With a slotted spoon transfer the pieces of meat to a large ovenproof casserole and arrange the vegetables over the top.

Pour the yogurt into a bowl and stir in the flour until well blended and smooth. Now stir in about 600 ml (1 pint) of the warm meat liquid from the saucepan and then pour the yogurt sauce into the casserole. Bring gently to the boil and simmer over a low heat for 10 minutes.

Pour the beaten eggs over the surface of the casserole and bake in the oven for 10–15 minutes until the egg is set and golden.

Remove from the oven, sprinkle with the garnishes and serve immediately.

ALI PAŞA KEBABI
Meat in Filo *Pastry*
——— • • • ———

A delicious meal of a light crisp pastry filled with a mixture of meat, onion and tomato.

Use *filo* pastry if possible. It can be bought from many continental and Middle Eastern shops, and from some supermarkets (see Glossary). Otherwise you can use either the dough used to make *Böreg Hamuru* (see p. 56) or else puff pastry – the frozen variety will do perfectly well.

Ali Paşa must surely have been a man of great refinement and taste – see also *Ali Paşa Pilavi*! (p. 31).

Serve with fresh vegetable salads and/or yogurt salads.

30 ml (2 tablespoons) butter or *ghee*
2 large onions, skinned and thinly sliced
900 g (2 lb) lean lamb, leg or shoulder
2 tomatoes, blanched, peeled and
    chopped
5 ml (1 teaspoon) salt
3.75 ml (¾ teaspoon) freshly ground
    black pepper

300 ml (½ pint) boiling water
30 ml (2 tablespoons) parsley, finely
    chopped

Pastry
12 sheets *filo* pastry – if using one of the
    other pastries suggested then 1
    thickness will do
50 g (2 oz) unsalted butter, melted

Melt the butter or *ghee* in a large saucepan, add the onion and fry for 5–10 minutes until soft and turning golden.

Cut the meat into 1-cm (½-inch) pieces and add to the saucepan. Cover the pan and simmer for about 5 minutes, stirring occasionally.

Add the tomatoes, salt, pepper and water and bring to the boil. Lower the heat and simmer for about 1 hour or until the meat is tender and most of the water has evaporated. Remove from the heat, stir in the parsley and set aside to cool. Heat the oven to 180°C (350°F) gas mark 4.

Meanwhile open up one sheet of the *filo* and brush it with melted butter. Place another sheet of *filo* over the top. Brush one half of this second sheet with butter and then fold the 2 sheets over so that they are half their original size.

Place ⅙ of the meat mixture in the centre of the *filo* and then fold the pastry over in envelope style to enclose the meat. Brush the edges with butter to hold them down and then brush the whole surface with butter. Continue with the remaining pastry and meat until you have 6 'parcels'.

Lightly grease 2 baking trays and place 3 parcels on each. Bake in the oven for 20–30 minutes or until the pastry is golden. Remove from the oven and serve with salads of your choice.

CHAPTER FIVE

BÖREKLER

Boregs

'If a woman cannot make a decent boreg – get rid of her.'

Boregs are small filled pies that come in many shapes – triangles, rolls, squares, semi-circles and so on. The name is probably derived from the Turkish word for kidney – *bobrek*.

These delectable pastries, though they do appear in other regions of the Middle East, are undoubtedly of Turkish origin since they are related to the numerous rice-paper dumplings of China and those of Russia – which are, in turn, of Mongolian Tartar origin.

The usual doughs are *filo*, flaky and shortcrust, but some boregs have their own dough. Boregs can be fried, boiled or baked. They are served as appetisers or savouries and can be eaten hot or cold.

SU BÖREĞI
Watered Pastry
——— · ● · ———

A classic of the Ottoman period. The ownership of this brilliant dish is hotly contested between Turks and Armenians. However, like many 'Turkish' dishes it evolved in Anatolia and not in the original homeland of the Turks. Also from personal observation I have noticed that this particular boreg appears far more often on Armenian tables than Turkish.

This recipe needs to be started the day before.

Pastry
6 eggs
5 ml (1 teaspoon) salt
10 ml (2 teaspoons) oil
450 g (1 lb) plain flour, sifted
Filling
450 g (1 lb) grated cheese

45 ml (3 tablespoons) chopped parsley
salt and pepper to taste
To Prepare
175 g (6 oz) butter, melted

Beat the eggs together in a large bowl and stir in the salt and oil. Stir in the flour and mix to a soft dough.

Transfer the dough to a floured work top and knead for several minutes until smooth and pliable.

Divide the dough into 12 portions and roll each into a ball. Place the balls, set well apart from each other, on a large baking tray and leave in a cool place overnight.

Grease an oblong tin about 20×25 cm (8×10 inches) and 5 cm (2 inches) deep.

Flour a work top and then roll each ball of dough out thinly to the shape of the tin. Set them aside.

In a very large saucepan bring about 7.2 litres (12 pints) water to the boil with 15 ml (1 tablespoon) salt. Fill another large pan with cold water.

Dip a sheet of dough into the boiling water and hold for about 30 seconds. Remove and dip immediately into the cold water. Dry on a tea towel and set aside.

Repeat with all the remaining sheets of dough.

Heat the oven to 200°C (400°F) gas mark 6.

Now prepare the filling by mixing the cheese and parsley together in a large bowl and season to taste with salt and pepper.

Place 2 sheets of the dough on top of each other in the tin. Pour a tablespoon of the melted butter over the second sheet. Lay 2 more sheets in the tin, again buttering the second sheet. Repeat with 2 more sheets of dough.

Spread the filling evenly over the 6th sheet.

Continue adding the sheets of dough and buttering every second one until they are all used up. Pour any remaining butter over the top sheet.

Place in the oven and bake for 30 minutes.

Remove from the oven and leave for 5 minutes. If you like it soft then cover for this 5 minutes, but if you prefer it crunchy then leave it open. Cut into 7.5-cm (3-inch) squares and serve warm.

BOHÇA BÖREĞI
Parcelled Boregs
—— • ● • ——

These round balls are baked in the oven and are usually served with fresh salads and pickles.

Pastry
1 large egg
200 ml (⅓ pint) yogurt
30 ml (2 tablespoons) olive oil
175 g (6 oz) butter, melted
350 g (12 oz) plain flour, sifted
5 ml (1 teaspoon) salt
5 ml (1 teaspoon) baking powder

Filling
100 g (4 oz) cream cheese *or* grated feta
2.5 ml (½ teaspoon) freshly ground
   black pepper
30 ml (2 tablespoons) chopped chives
30 ml (2 tablespoons) chopped parsley
60 ml (2 fl oz) milk

Place the egg, yogurt and oil in a large bowl and whisk until well blended. Gradually add the flour, salt and baking powder and stir in to form a smooth dough. Cover the bowl with a clean tea towel and refrigerate for 30 minutes.

Meanwhile in a bowl mix the cheese, pepper, chives and parsley.

Break off a walnut-sized lump of dough and roll it between your palms to form a smooth ball. Push an index finger into the centre and hollow it out a little. Place a teaspoonful of the cheese mixture in the centre and then close up the hole. Roll it between your palms again to regain its round shape. Continue until all the pastry and filling have been used up.

Heat the oven to 200°C (400°F) gas mark 6.

Lightly grease 2 large baking trays and arrange the balls on them about 5 cm (2 inches) apart. Brush with the milk and bake in the oven for 20–25 minutes or until golden.

BÖREG HAMURU
Pastry for Boreg

'I didn't whiten my beard in a flour mill.'
– I am aged with experience.
—— • ● • ——

This method of preparing dough is the traditional one and, although it does take some time, it is not very difficult and is deliciously soft and flaky. You can, of course, use commercial puff pastry with very successful results.

450 g (1 lb) plain flour
5 ml (1 teaspoon) salt
240 ml (8 fl oz) cold water
5 ml (1 teaspoon) lemon juice

50 g (2 oz) clarified butter or *ghee*,
   melted
225 g (8 oz) block of margarine or
   butter, chilled

Sift the flour and salt into a large bowl. Make a well in the centre, add the water and lemon juice and mix thoroughly, using a wooden spoon.

Add the melted, clarified butter or *ghee* and knead for 10 minutes until smooth. Shape the dough into a large ball, cover with a damp cloth and leave for 30 minutes.

Lightly flour a work top and roll out the dough until ½ cm (¼ inch) thick. Put the block of margarine or butter in the middle of the dough and fold the pastry over the fat so that it is completely enclosed. With a well-floured rolling pin, flatten the dough to a 1 cm (½ inch) thickness. Fold the dough in half and refrigerate for 10 minutes.

Return the dough to the floured work top and roll out to ½ cm (¼ inch) thickness. Fold in half and refrigerate for a further 10 minutes.

Keeping the work top well floured, roll out the dough once more as thinly as possible. Now cut into the desired sizes and shapes for the boreg you are preparing and continue with the relevant recipe.

ISPANAKLI BÖREĞI
Spinach Boreg
———— • ● • ————

This is a popular boreg filled with spinach, which uses the boreg pastry opposite.

Pastry
One quantity of *Böreg Hamuru* (see opposite)
Filling
450 g (1 lb) spinach, washed very thoroughly under cold running water
90 ml (6 tablespoons) olive oil
1 small onion, skinned and finely chopped

5 ml (1 teaspoon) salt
2.5 ml (½ teaspoon) freshly ground black pepper
juice of 1 lemon
Glaze
1 egg, beaten

Prepare the pastry following the relevant instructions.

To prepare the filling discard any coarse spinach leaves and stems. Bring a large saucepan half filled with lightly salted water to the boil. Add the spinach and simmer for 5–8 minutes. Strain into a colander. When cool enough to handle squeeze out as much water as possible and then chop.

Preheat the oven to 190°C (350°F) gas mark 5.

Heat the oil in a saucepan, add the onion and fry for 5–10 minutes until soft and lightly browned. Add the spinach, salt and pepper and cook over a low heat, stirring occasionally, for about 5 minutes. Stir in the lemon juice and set aside to cool.

Roll the dough out thinly and cut into 10-cm (4-inch) squares. Place 10 ml (2 teaspoonfuls) of the filling in the centre of one half of each square. Dampen the edges of the pastry and fold over to form a triangle. Seal the edges with the prongs of a fork.

Arrange the boreg on 2 large greased baking trays and brush with beaten egg. Bake in the oven for about 20 minutes or until golden. Arrange on a large dish and serve hot.

ÇERKEZ PUF BÖREĞI
Minced Meat Boreg

—— • ● • ——

A favourite of the Circassians of the Caucasus, famed for their beautiful women and their war-loving men.

These are delightful pastries which are fried in oil. The dough used in this recipe is a Middle Eastern version of puff pastry. The usual filling is that of minced meat and onion, but sometimes this is replaced by fillings of cheese or brains.

These make excellent starters or, when served with salads, a filling lunch or supper.

Filling
15 ml (1 tablespoon) butter
1 small onion, skinned and finely
  chopped
450 g (1 lb) lamb or beef, minced twice.
  You can use beef instead
45 ml (3 tablespoons) parsley, finely
  chopped
5 ml (1 teaspoon) salt
2.5 ml (½ teaspoon) freshly ground
  black pepper

Pastry
450 g (1 lb) plain flour
5 ml (1 teaspoon) salt
2 egg yolks
15 ml (1 tablespoon) yogurt
60 ml (4 tablespoons) olive oil
2.5 ml (½ teaspoon) lemon juice
about 120 ml (4 fl oz) milk
50–75 g (2–3 oz) butter, melted
To Fry
oil

First prepare the filling by melting the butter in a saucepan. Add the onion and fry for 5 minutes until soft. Stir in the minced meat, parsley, salt and pepper and fry for 20–30 minutes or until the meat is well cooked. Remove from the heat and leave to cool while you prepare the dough.

Sift the flour and salt into a large bowl. Make a well in the centre and add the egg yolks, yogurt, oil and lemon juice. Mix together with a wooden spoon and then knead for about 10 minutes, adding a little milk at a time until you have a soft, smooth dough. Shape it into a large ball and dust with flour.

Sprinkle a working surface with flour and, breaking off walnut-sized lumps, roll each one out as thinly as possible into circles about 20 cm (8 inches) in diameter. Continue until you have used all the dough.

Brush the upper surface of one circle of dough with melted butter, place another circle of dough on top of it and brush its upper surface with the butter. Continue stacking the circles of dough in this way, brushing each upper surface with butter, until they form one pile.

Liberally sprinkle the working surface and rolling pin with flour and roll out the pile of dough circles until you have one large sheet of dough which is very thin. Cover with a clean cloth and leave to rest for 30 minutes.

Cut the pastry into 10-cm (4-inch) squares and place 10 ml (a dessertspoonful) of the filling in the centre of each square. Dampen the edges of the pastry and either

a) fold into a triangle, pinching the edges with your thumbs or a fork to seal or
b) spread the filling in a ridge about 1 cm (½ inch) from one edge and then fold the edge over it, turn in the two sides and roll out into a cigarette shape.
Continue until you have used up all the dough and filling.

Heat sufficient oil in a large pan to deep fry and, when hot enough, fry the boreg, a few at a time, until golden and heated through. Remove with a slotted spoon, drain on kitchen paper and serve hot.

ADAPAZAR BÖREĞI

Milk and Yogurt Boreg

'One hand in butter, the other in honey.'
– A rich man.

—— • • • ——

A delicious boreg from Adapazar – 'Island Bazaar' – which used to be an important trading town with silk, tobacco and walnut wood factories. There is situated the famed 1,400-foot long stone bridge built by the Emperor Justinian which is still defying time.

This boreg can be served in small pieces as an appetiser or, in larger pieces, as a main course. If you wish you can use sheets of *filo* pastry for this boreg instead of making the dough suggested.

Pastry
225 g (½ lb) plain flour, sifted
2.5 ml (½ teaspoon) salt
1 egg
about 150 ml (¼ pint) milk
Filling
100 g (4 oz) white cheese – if using feta
  soak it in water for 2–4 hours,
  changing the water twice

30 ml (2 tablespoons) yogurt
1 egg
30–45 ml (2–3 tablespoons) milk
To Prepare
30–45 ml (2–3 tablespoons) cornflour
100 g (4 oz) clarified butter or *ghee*,
  melted
a little boiling water

To prepare the dough place the flour and salt in a mixing bowl. Make a well in the centre, add the egg and milk and mix with a wooden spoon. Transfer to a work top dusted with cornflour and knead until you have a soft, pliable dough.

Divide the dough into 14 equal portions and roll each into a ball. Roll each ball in a little cornflour and set aside while you prepare the filling.

Crumble the cheese into a bowl, add the yogurt, egg, milk and black pepper and mix well. Grease a cake tin or tray about 20 cm (8 inches) in diameter. Heat the oven to 180°C (350°F) gas mark 4.

Lightly sprinkle a worktop with cornflour and then take 1 ball of dough and roll it out from the centre to the edges to give it a circular shape, until it is paper thin. Arrange the sheet of dough over the base of the tin and brush it all over with melted butter. Roll out another 6 balls and place each one in the tin on top of the other, brushing the surface of each with melted butter.

Spread the filling evenly over the 7th sheet, but do not press it down.

Continue rolling out the balls of dough, arranging them in the tin and brushing each with melted butter. Pour any remaining butter over the top sheet.

Bake in the oven for 35–40 minutes or until golden.

Remove from the oven and brush the surface with some boiling water. Cover with a tea towel and leave for 15 minutes. Cut into wedges and serve warm.

YAGLI PEYNIRLI BÖREĞI
Cheese-Filled Pastries

—— • • ——

These are probably the most popular savoury boreg. There are many variations of this filling and I have included below two typical ones.

These boreg can be made very successfully with commercial puff pastry, but I would suggest that you try your own and follow the recipe for *Böreg Hamuru*.

Served with salad these will make a pleasant and filling meal.

Pastry
One quantity of *Böreg Hamuru* (see p. 56)

Filling 1
275 g (10 oz) soft white cheese, grated or crumbled
1 egg, beaten
45 ml (3 tablespoons) finely chopped parsley
2.5 ml (½ teaspoon) salt – if using feta, taste before adding any, it may be salty enough
2.5 ml (½ teaspoon) black pepper

Filling 2 – an Istanbul favourite
275 g (10 oz) grated cheese e.g. cheddar
1 egg, beaten
75–90 ml (5–6 tablespoons) milk
10 ml (2 teaspoons) oregano
1.25 ml (¼ teaspoon) white pepper

Garnish
1 egg, beaten
30 ml (2 tablespoons) dried mint *or* sesame seeds

Prepare the dough following the relevant instructions.

Preheat the oven to 190°C (375°F) gas mark 5.

Prepare the filling of your choice by placing all the ingredients in a bowl and mixing well.

Roll the dough out thinly and cut into 10-cm (4-inch) squares.

Place a heaped teaspoonful of the filling in the centre of one half of each square. Dampen the edges of the pastry with cold water and fold over to form a triangle. Seal the edges with the prongs of a fork.

Brush the top of each triangle with beaten egg and sprinkle with either the dried mint or the sesame seeds.

Arrange on greased baking trays and cook in the oven for about 20 minutes or until the boreg have risen and are golden. Serve hot.

TARTAR BÖREĞI
Chicken Boreg
· ● ·

As the name suggests this is a classic of Tartar origin. The Tartars, of course, were 'Turks' from Central Asia. They have virtually disappeared as a nation, having been assimilated by the Russians.

The other famous dish of the warring tribes who terrorised the whole of Asia for generations is, of course, Steak Tartar.

Pastry
450 g (1 lb) plain flour
2 eggs, beaten
120 ml (4 fl oz) milk
Filling
50 g (1 oz) butter
15 ml (1 tablespoon) flour
300 ml (½ pint) chicken stock
350 g (12 oz) cooked chicken breast, chopped
5 ml (1 teaspoon) salt

1.25 ml (¼ teaspoon) freshly ground black pepper
1.25 ml (¼ teaspoon) marjoram
50 g (2 oz) white cheese, grated
Glaze
50 g (2 oz) butter, melted
Sauce
15 ml (1 tablespoon) butter
15 ml (1 tablespoon) tomato purée
120 ml (4 fl oz) water
50 g (2 oz) grated cheese

Sift the flour into a large bowl and make a well in the centre. Add the eggs and mix. Slowly add the milk and knead until you have a soft, smooth dough which is pliable. Cover with a cloth and leave to rest while you prepare the filling.

Preheat the oven to 180°C (350°F) gas mark 4.

Melt the butter in a saucepan them remove from the heat and stir in the flour. Gradually stir in the stock, return to the heat and cook gently until the sauce thickens, stirring constantly. Remove from the heat and stir in the chicken, salt, pepper, marjoram and cheese.

Lightly flour a working top and roll out the pastry as thinly as possible. Cut the pastry into 10-cm (4-inch) squares.

Brush each square with some of the melted butter. Place a walnut-sized lump of the filling in the centre of each square and then roll up and seal the ends securely with the prongs of a fork.

Arrange on lightly greased baking trays and brush the tops with the remaining melted butter. Bake in the oven for 20–30 minutes or until golden.

Meanwhile place all the sauce ingredients in a saucepan and cook over a low heat for 2–3 minutes.

Remove the boreg from the oven, place on a serving dish, pour the sauce over them and serve.

CHAPTER SIX

YEMEKLER
Main Dishes

'Be little lambs,
they tell us
So that when you grow up
We can lead you like sheep.'
CAN YUCEL

In Turkey lamb is synonymous with meat – very much like pork is in China. There is little local beef or veal and hardly any pork, which is prohibited by religious dogmas. Lamb dominates the kitchen and has, over the centuries, created an enviable repertoire. Indeed, one of the most outstanding characteristics of both Turkish and Middle Eastern cuisines is the many wonderful ways of cooking lamb; perhaps the finest in all the cuisines of the world. The doner kebab, for example, the vertical spit kebab, has acquired prominence throughout the Middle East and in most large European cities.

Naturally other meats and poultry are used, and so are fish which come in a splendid variety. Turkey has a vast length of coastline and the warm waters of the Mediterranean and Black Seas are well endowed with the finest quality red and grey mullet, swordfish, mackerel, mussels, prawns, sardines, haddock, lobsters and more. Turks like to eat their fish simply, usually deep-fried in oil with a few drops of lemon juice squeezed over them – and perhaps a glass of *raki*.

However, we open this chapter with what is probably the most famous of all the Middle Eastern dishes:

ŞIŞ KEBABI
Skewered Chunks of Meat

———— •●• ————

This is, in essence, a very simple dish consisting of meat and onions marinated in oil and spices.

This, and similar kebabs cooked over charcoal, originated in the Caucasus and subsequently spread southwards to the other Mediterranean lands. Traditionally the meat used is lamb and, specifically, the leg. In order to achieve a perfect kebab 3 basic points must be noted –

 a) all tough membranes and ligaments must be removed
 b) the meat must be cut across the grain
 c) the meat must be marinated

Below are 3 marinades popular in Turkey.

900 g (2 lb) leg of lamb, cut into 2.5-cm (1-inch) pieces
1 large onion, skinned and quartered and separated into layers

Marinade 1
150 ml (¼ pint) olive oil
2 onions, skinned, then chopped and crushed in a garlic press to extract juice
5 ml (1 teaspoon) cinnamon
5 ml (1 teaspoon) salt
2.5 ml (½ teaspoon) freshly ground black pepper

Marinade 2
300 ml (½ pint) yogurt
juice of 1 onion, skinned, chopped and crushed to extract the juice
5 ml (1 teaspoon) salt
2.5 ml (½ teaspoon) freshly ground black pepper

Marinade 3
150 ml (¼ pint) olive oil
juice of 1 lemon
2 bay leaves
5 ml (1 teaspoon) oregano

Put all the ingredients for the marinade of your choice in a large bowl and mix well. Add the cubes of meat, turn until they are well coated with the marinade and refrigerate for about 8 hours or overnight.

When ready to cook thread the pieces of meat, interspersed with layers of onion, on to skewers. Grill, preferably over charcoal, turning occasionally, for 10–15 minutes or until the meat is cooked and brown on the outside, but still a little pink and moist inside.

Serve with a rice *pilav* of your choice and a fresh salad.

SAHAN KEBABI
Shish Kebab with Vegetables

———— • ● • ————

Here the shish kebab is served with cooked vegetables and fried bread. You can prepare and serve this sauce with other kinds of kebabs.

Meat and Marinade
see recipe for *Şiş Kebabi*
Vegetables
3 medium aubergines
30 ml (2 tablespoons) margarine
45 ml (3 tablespoons) butter
1 large onion, skinned and finely chopped
4 large tomatoes, blanched, peeled, seeded and chopped

2.5 ml (½ teaspoon) salt
300 ml (½ pint) yogurt
30 ml (2 tablespoons) parsley or coriander, finely chopped
Bread
3 pita breads, cut into 2-cm (¾-inch) wide strips
15 ml (1 tablespoon) butter
45 ml (3 tablespoons) water

Prepare and cook the meat as described in the last recipe.

Meanwhile make 2 or 3 slits in each aubergine with a sharp knife and cook them either in a hot oven, under the grill or over charcoal until the skins are black and the flesh soft when poked with a finger.

When cool enough to handle peel off the skin, scraping away and reserving any flesh that comes away with the skin. Put the flesh into a bowl and mash with a fork. Set aside.

Melt the margarine and butter in a frying pan, add the onion and fry until soft, stirring occasionally. Add the tomatoes and salt and fry for a further 5 minutes, stirring regularly. Spoon out and reserve 45 ml (3 tablespoons) of the melted fat in the pan. Add the reserved aubergine flesh to the pan, mix well and fry for 2–3 minutes. Remove from the heat and reserve.

Melt the 15 ml (tablespoon) of butter in a pan, add the strips of bread and fry for a few minutes, turning occasionally. Pour the 45 ml (3 tablespoons) water over the bread, cover the pan and remove from the heat.

When the kebabs are done divide the fried bread between 6 plates and arrange the aubergine mixture over it. Spoon the yogurt over the vegetables and then place the kebabs on top. Sprinkle a little of the reserved melted butter over each and garnish with some parsley.

URFA KEBABI
Aubergine and Meat Kebab

———— • ● • ————

Urfa is a city in Southern Turkey with not too much to show for thousands of years of history (it used to be known as Edessa) except perhaps for this dish and a few other meat dishes, mainly stews and roasts.

My father used to say that the best things about Urfa were the chilli peppers and apple-tasting aubergines. The rest, all of it, could go into the stew!

900 g (2 lb) lamb or beef, minced twice
2 onions, skinned and very finely
  chopped
2 eggs, beaten

7.5 ml (1½ teaspoons) salt
2.5 ml (½ teaspoon) freshly ground
  black pepper
4 medium-sized aubergines

Put the minced meat, onions, eggs, salt and pepper into a large bowl and knead for about 5 minutes until well blended and very smooth. Keeping your hands damp with warm water, take walnut-sized lumps of meat and roll into balls.

Cut the heads off the aubergines and then slice into 1-cm (½-inch) thick rings. Thread the meatballs on to skewers alternating with aubergine slices.

Cook over charcoal for 10–15 minutes. The aubergines may take a little longer to cook than the meat and so make sure that they are tender.

Serve with rice and a salad.

Variation
ADANA KEBABI
Adana Kebab
———— • • • ————

Probably the most exciting food found in Turkey today comes from the region of Çukurova (Armenian Cilicia), in which Adana is the major city. The Adana kebab is a well-known spicy version of the above, without the aubergines.

Prepare the meat as described above but add 100 g (4 oz) *kuyruk yagi* – the fat from the tail of a sheep (you can use shredded suet instead) – and 2 finely chopped green chilli peppers.

Cook and serve as with *Urfa Kebabi*.

TANDIR KEBAB
Lamb Cooked in a Pit
'*When an ox falls – men sharpen their knives.*'
———— • • • ————

This is one of the oldest forms of cooking. *Tandir* (related to the Indian *Tandoor*) is a shallow, 60–90 cm (2–3 foot) pit in which is laid a bed of charcoal. The whole lamb is laid on the charcoal and the pit is then filled in with earth so that the lamb is completely covered.

The baking process takes about 5–6 hours. When ready the lamb is removed, brushed to remove soil and clinging charcoal and then placed on a large tray. The tray is shaken until the meat drops from the bones on to the tray. The bones are removed and the meat is sprinkled with salt, black pepper and thyme. Meat cooked in this way is extremely soft, tender and moist. Potatoes and chestnuts are often cooked with the lamb and the whole is served with *pilavs*, salads and pickles. It makes an extremely exotic picnic.

ŞIŞ KOFTESI
Minced Meat on Skewers

*'Abi (brother), he is a veritable fool. He is
teaching an Armenian how to cook kebabs.'*
– A little like 'teaching your grandmother to suck eggs.'

Basically there are two kinds of kebabs, one made with chunks of meat, the other with minced meat. The former is more popular with Armenians, Caucasians and Turks, the latter with Persians and Arabs. Having said this I hasten to add that this is a generalisation and the finest *Şiş Koftesi* come from Urfa and Gaziantep, while the ones from Mardin in southern Turkey tend to be the hottest with the red chilli peppers competing with the redness of the meat.

I have given 3 recipes for this dish, which can be considered the hamburger of the east.

Istanbul Version
900 g (2 lb) lamb, minced twice
2 eggs
2.5 ml (½ teaspoon) thyme
5ml (1 teaspoon) salt
1 garlic clove, skinned and crushed
1 large onion, skinned and grated
2.5 ml (½ teaspoon) white pepper

Anatolian Version
900 g (2 lb) lamb or beef, minced twice
2 onions, skinned and very finely
  chopped
2 eggs
7.5 ml (1½ teaspoons) salt

2.5 ml (½ teaspoon) freshly ground
  black pepper

Mardin-Kurdish Version
900 g (2 lb) lamb or goat meat, minced
  twice
2 onions, skinned and very finely
  chopped
30 ml (2 tablespoons) parsley, finely
  chopped
1½ chilli peppers, or more to taste
1 garlic clove, skinned and crushed
5 ml (1 teaspoon) salt
2.5 ml (½ teaspoon) freshly ground
  black pepper

Place all the ingredients for the version of your choice in a large bowl. Keeping your hands damp, knead until the mixture is smooth and pliable like a dough. Break off an egg-sized lump and pass a skewer through it. Still keeping your hands damp, squeeze the meat firmly out along the skewer until it is thin and sausage-shaped. Repeat with the remaining mixture.

Place on a well-oiled grid and cook over charcoal for 8–10 minutes or until cooked through.

KUZU KEBABI or KUZU CEVIRME
Whole Lamb Cooked over Charcoal

This is by far the most sumptuous kebab of all. A whole lamb, rinsed out, with eyes blackened or removed and with a piece of confectionery or an apple placed in the mouth, has a metal or wooden rod pushed through it from breast bone to hindquarters. Its legs are trussed and it is then cooked over charcoal. The Turks celebrate their holy days of Bayram by sacrificing a whole lamb and cooking it with its head turned towards Mecca.

Lambs are slaughtered for weddings, anniversaries, at the birth of a child – particularly a boy. This sacrificial tradition is a very old one, pre-Muslim and pre-Christian and dates from the 'sacrifice of the first-born' that ancient man practised.

You too can partake of this exotic and quasi-religious meal if money and space permit and, with this in mind, I have given below a standard recipe.

 bout 12–14 kg (25–30 lb), entrails removed.

: lamb inside and out and wipe dry. Rub inside and out with salt, black pepper and some onion juice.

Push a rod through the lamb, truss the legs and cook over a wood or charcoal fire. This is normally laid in a shallow pit and other kebabs, as well as sauces, are cooked on it at the same time.

Baste frequently and cook for at least 4 hours, turning occasionally.

Serve with rice *pilavs*, salads, yogurt drinks and bread.

A MATTER OF SIZE

One day the Hodja had bought a lamb for the Muslim festival of Sacrifice, Bayram. He meant to fatten it until Bayram which was due in about 8 weeks. The lamb was co-operating well when one day it disappeared. The poor Hodja left no stone unturned to find it, but all was in vain. A few days later he learned that it was his own lamb that had been served at the party given by one of his neighbours at which he had been a guest himself. The Hodja took his revenge by giving a party himself and serving one of the kids of the angora goat belonging to that same neighbour. But, unlike the Hodja, who had suffered the loss of his lamb in silence, his neighbour kept lamenting the loss of his angora kid for weeks on end. Furthermore, the size of the kid (which had originally been that of a medium-sized cat) kept growing alarmingly. When it had become as large as a cow the Hodja could stand it no longer. He rushed home and was back in no time with the hide of the kid in his hand. Holding it up for everyone to see, he cried, 'Oh good people, here is the hide of the kid my neighbour has been pestering us about for the past three weeks! Judge for yourselves if it will fit a creature the size of a cow!'

TAVUK KEBABI
Chicken Kebab
———— • ● • ————

There is very little 'chicken farming' in Turkey – lucky them, and the poultry available, although not as plump and meaty as their American and European counterparts, has much more flavour. Chicken meat is, after lamb, the most popular, and in recent years *piliç* (poussins) have also gained favour.

Turks like to picnic, and chicken kebab is one of the 'stars' of such happy events.

Marinate the chicken before cooking as the flesh easily absorbs the different flavours of the marinades, bastes or sauces. Given below are 2 Turkish marinades.

You can grill the chicken whole, halved, or cut into 8 serving pieces – 2 breasts, 2 wings, 2 drumsticks and 2 thighs. You can also use ready-prepared chicken pieces.

Marinade 1	*Marinade 2*
150 ml (¼ pint) olive oil	150 ml (¼ pint) olive oil
3 garlic cloves, skinned and finely chopped	juice of 2 lemons
juice of 1 lemon	2 garlic cloves, skinned and finely chopped
5 ml (1 teaspoon) salt	10 ml (2 teaspoons) oregano
2.5 ml (½ teaspoon) white pepper	2.5 ml (½ teaspoon) chilli pepper
	5 ml (1 teaspoon) salt

Put the marinade ingredients of your choice in a large bowl and mix well. Add the whole chicken or chicken pieces and turn until well coated with the marinade. Set aside at room temperature for 2–3 hours.

Thread on to skewers and cook over charcoal. Use any remaining marinade to baste the chicken while it is cooking to prevent the flesh drying out.

KADIN BUDU
Lady's Thigh Kofta
———— • ● • ————

Lady's thigh *kofta* should be round, soft and smooth!

A very simple, popular dish, this is one of many clever ways Turkish housewives make use of minced meat. Serve hot with rice or spaghetti, salads and/or pickles.

675 g (1½ lb) lamb, minced twice	7.5 ml (1½ teaspoons) salt
1 large onion, skinned and finely chopped	2.5 ml (½ teaspoon) freshly ground black pepper
175 g (6 oz) cooked rice	7.5 ml (1½ teaspoons) ground cumin
45 ml (3 tablespoons) white cheese, grated	*To cook*
1 egg	oil for frying
25 g (1 oz) flour	1–2 eggs, beaten

Place all the ingredients in a large bowl and knead for several minutes until the mixture is well blended and smooth. Keeping your hands damp take a walnut-sized lump and roll it into a ball. Flatten it gently by pressing it between your palms. Place on a baking tray and prepare the remaining meat mixture in the same way.

Heat some oil in a large frying pan. Dip a few of the *kofta* at a time in beaten egg and fry, turning occasionally, until cooked through and golden. Remove with a slotted spoon, arrange on a serving dish and keep warm while you cook the remaining *kofta* in the same way.

Tavşan Kebabı
Rabbit Kebab

'Rabbit – to see; crudity; unpleasant behaviour. Rabbits fighting – shortsightedness; court action; forced possession. To eat rabbit meat – the fulfilment of all efforts and triumphal success. To cook rabbit – wealth and fame.'

from a 19TH-CENTURY BOOK OF DREAMS

— • • • —

As well as being a relatively cheap meat it is also worth preparing this dish if it will bestow on you some of the above mentioned qualities. This is a particularly succulent way of cooking rabbit and is of Anatolian origin.

1 rabbit, skinned, cleaned and washed inside and out. Reserve the liver.
3 garlic cloves, skinned and halved lengthways
6 cloves

Marinade
150 ml (¼ pint) olive oil
5 ml (1 teaspoon) mint
3 bay leaves, crumbled
5 ml (1 teaspoon) chopped tarragon
30 ml (2 tablespoons) parsley, finely chopped

Sauce
50 g (2 oz) butter
2 garlic gloves, skinned and chopped
150 ml (¼ pint) red wine
juice of 1 lemon
5 ml (1 teaspoon) salt
2.5 ml (½ teaspoon) freshly ground black pepper
2.5 ml (½ teaspoon) allspice

SERVES 4

When the rabbit is clean and dry make small incisions all over the body with a sharp knife. Stud the garlic halves and cloves into the incisions.

Mix the marinade ingredients together in a large dish, add the rabbit and turn to coat with the marinade. Cover and refrigerate overnight, or for several hours.

Remove the rabbit from the dish, drain and thread on a spit or 2 skewers. Reserve the marinade. Cook over charcoal for 1–1½ hours, basting frequently with the marinade as you turn the rabbit.

Meanwhile prepare the sauce by melting in a small saucepan. Add the reserved liver and the garlic and fry for 3–4 minutes, stirring frequently. Remove from the heat and stir in the remaining sauce ingredients before returning to the heat and bringing to simmering point.

Transfer the rabbit to a serving plate, carve, pour the sauce over and serve.

SÜLÜN DOLMA KEBABI
Pheasants Stuffed with Nuts

Pious as a pheasant,
Proud as a peacock,
But mean, oh as mean as a vulture
Was my love.

KURDISH FOLK SONG

— • • • —

Turks love this bird which is found in abundance in the countryside. This recipe is for a pheasant stuffed with liver and nuts and grilled over charcoal. It is extremely attractive in appearance and flavour. Serve with salad, yogurt and a *pilav* of your choice.

2 young pheasants, hung
Stuffing
175 g (6 oz) mixed walnuts and
   pistachios, chopped
600 ml (1 pint) chicken stock
100 g (4 oz) butter
450 g (1 lb) chicken livers, finely
   chopped

175 g (6 oz) raisins
5 ml (1 teaspoon) salt
2.5 ml (½ teaspoon) chilli pepper
2.5 ml (½ teaspoon) allspice
Garnish
lemon wedges

Clean out the pheasants, wash inside and out, dry and set aside.

Now prepare the stuffing by first simmering the nuts in the stock until they are tender and most of the liquid has evaporated.

Melt half the butter in a small saucepan and fry the chopped livers for a few minutes. Add this to the nut mixture together with the remaining ingredients.

Stuff the pheasants with this mixture and then truss them, thread on to a spit or skewers and cook over charcoal for about 1 hour, turning frequently and basting with the remaining butter which you have melted.

Serve on a large plate with the lemon wedges.

KILIC ŞIŞTE
Swordfish Kebab

— • • • —

This famed kebab, popular in all the seaside restaurants of Istanbul, has the fish grilled with bay leaves which gives the flesh a delightful flavour.

It is traditionally served with a plain rice *pilav* and *Tarator* Sauce – (see p. 94).

900 g (2 lb) swordfish
1 onion, skinned and cut into 1-cm
   (½-inch) thick slices and separated
   into rings
45 ml (3 tablespoons) lemon juice
30 ml (2 tablespoons) olive oil
5 ml (1 teaspoon) paprika

7.5 ml (1½ teaspoons) salt
2.5 ml (½ teaspoon) freshly ground
   black pepper
20 large bay leaves
Garnish
30 ml (2 tablespoons) parsley, finely
   chopped

Skin and bone the fish and cut the flesh into 2.5-cm (1-inch) cubes.

Put the onion in a large bowl with 25 ml (1½ tablespoons) of the lemon juice, 15 ml (1 tablespoon) of the olive oil, the paprika, salt and pepper and mix well. Add the fish cubes and toss to coat thoroughly with the marinade. Leave to marinate for at least 4 hours.

Meanwhile soak the bay leaves in a little boiling water for about 1 hour and then drain.

Remove the fish from the marinade and thread on to skewers, alternating each piece with a bay leaf. Press firmly together so that the flavour passes from the leaves to the fish.

Mix the remaining oil and lemon juice together and brush the kebabs with this baste. Cook over charcoal for about 10 minutes, turning and basting occasionally until the fish is golden.

Slide the fish off the skewers on to a bed of plain rice *pilav* and serve with some *Tarator* Sauce.

BURSA TAVUKI
Chicken with Herbs
— • • —

Bursa (Prusa ad Olympium) is a prosperous city at the foot of Mount Olympus which still retains a great deal of its medieval charm and dirt! It is one of the most 'Turkish' of all Turkish cities, with the colour green dominating all others.

There are several fine local dishes whose reputation has spread beyond the fortified ancient city walls. This recipe for chicken with herbs is one of them. It is usually served with a rice *pilav* of your choice and a salad.

1 large chicken cut into 6 serving pieces
or 6 ready-prepared chicken pieces
75 ml (5 tablespoons) olive oil
2 onions, skinned and thinly sliced
450 ml (¾ pint) chicken stock or water
2.5 ml (½ teaspoon) marjoram
2.5 ml (½ teaspoon) basil
2.5 ml (½ teaspoon) tarragon

2.5 ml (½ teaspoon) salt
2.5 ml (½ teaspoon) white pepper
15 ml (1 tablespoon) plain flour
45 ml (3 tablespoons) single cream
50 g (2 oz) stuffed green olives
Garnish
15 ml (1 tablespoon) parsley, finely chopped

Heat the oil in a large casserole. Add the chicken pieces, 2 or 3 at a time, and fry until lightly browned, turning once. Remove and reserve.

Add the onions to the casserole and fry, stirring frequently, until golden. Return the chicken pieces and add the stock, marjoram, basil, tarragon, salt and pepper. Bring to the boil and then lower the heat, cover the pan and simmer for about 1 hour or until the chicken is tender.

Remove the chicken pieces to a serving dish and keep warm.

In a small bowl blend the flour and cream until smooth. Stir in a few tablespoons of the hot sauce and then stir this mixture into the sauce. Add the olives and simmer for a few minutes, stirring constantly.

To serve, pour the sauce over the chicken pieces and sprinkle with the parsley.

BALUK KEBABI
Fish Kebab

·•·

Fish is excellent either grilled whole or in steaks, fillets or chunks. Most fish lend themselves to this kind of cooking and I have listed below 3 marinades which are popular in Turkey.

As fish flakes when it is cooked it is usually advisable to cook larger pieces such as steaks, fillets or whole fish in an oiled double grill as this makes it easier to turn without breaking.

Serve with a rice *pilav* or salad.

6 portions fish, either steaks or small whole fish (use firm fish, like halibut, trout, mullet)

Olive Oil Marinade
90 ml (6 tablespoons) olive oil
5 ml (1 teaspoon) oregano
5 ml (1 teaspoon) salt
2.5 ml (½ teaspoon) freshly ground black pepper

Yogurt Marinade
50 g (2 oz) butter or *ghee*, melted
300 ml (½ pint) yogurt
5 ml (1 teaspoon) salt
5 ml (1 teaspoon) coriander
1.25 ml (¼ teaspoon) cardamom
1.25 ml (¼ teaspoon) freshly ground black pepper

30 ml (2 tablespoons) lemon juice

Garlic Marinade
90 ml (6 tablespoons) olive oil
90 ml (6 tablespoons) lemon juice
2 garlic cloves, skinned and crushed
5 ml (1 teaspoon) salt
2.5 ml (½ teaspoon) freshly ground black pepper
2.5 ml (½ teaspoon) coriander

Garnish
30 ml (2 tablespoons) parsley, fennel or dill, freshly chopped
lemon wedges
spring onions

Clean, wash and dry the fish.

Mix all the ingredients of the marinade of your choice in a large, shallow dish. Add the pieces of fish, turn several times to coat well, cover and refrigerate overnight, or for several hours.

When ready to cook remove from the marinade, put into a double grill and cook over charcoal for 10–20 minutes depending on the thickness of the fish, turning regularly.

Garnish with herbs, and serve with lemon wedges and spring onions.

KILIS KUSLARI

Meat and Nuts in Lamb

• • •

This dish is very popular in southern Turkey, particularly in the Gaziantep, Kilis, Urfa and Iskenderun regions where a great number of Arabs still live and where a much stronger Arabic influence still exists. This dish is of Syrian origin and it is very tasty and attractive and makes an ideal choice for a dinner party. As well as this I have also included it out of filial duty for not only was it one of my father's favourites, but it also bears the name of the town where he was born.

Serve with a *pilav* and/or salad of your choice.

8 slices of lamb, leg or shoulder, flattened to ½ cm (¼ inch) thickness and trimmed into approx. 12.5 × 12.5-cm (5 × 5-inch) squares

Stuffing

30 ml (2 tablespoons) butter
1 onion, skinned and finely chopped
450 g (1 lb) minced lamb
2 tomatoes, blanched, peeled and chopped
45 ml (3 tablespoons) walnuts, chopped
15 ml (1 tablespoon) parsley, finely chopped

5 ml (1 teaspoon) salt
2.5 ml (½ teaspoon) allspice

Sauce

15 ml (1 tablespoon) tomato purée
300 ml (½ pint) water
2 garlic cloves, skinned and finely chopped
3 bay leaves

Garnish

lemon wedges

SERVES 8

Melt the butter in a saucepan, add the onion and fry gently for 5 minutes until soft. Add the meat and fry for 10 minutes, stirring frequently to break up the lumps. Remove from the heat and set aside to cool.

Prepare the slices of lamb as described and then lay the slices out flat.

Put about 30 ml (2 tablespoons) of the filling in the centre of one slice and then roll the meat up and secure with 1 or 2 cocktail sticks. If any of the stuffing oozes out of the ends then push it back with your finger. Continue until you have made up 8 rolls.

Pack the rolls into a shallow baking dish.

Mix all the sauce ingredients together in a bowl and pour over the meat rolls.

Place in an oven preheated to 350°F (180°C) gas mark 4 and cook for about 1 hour or until the lamb is tender, basting with the sauce occasionally.

Remove from the oven, lift out the rolls and arrange on a serving dish. Either spoon the sauce over the top or serve separately.

MANTI
Dumplings with Meat
———— • • • ————

This dish of meat-filled dumplings is Mongolian in origin and is one of the few truly Mongolian-Turkish dishes that is found in Turkey today. It is the national dish of Mongolia, is very popular in Korea, is related to the steamed rice bread dishes of China (*mant'ou*) and to the dumpling dishes of Uzbekistan and Turkmenistan.

Today in Turkey there are two popular versions – one with a tomato sauce and another with a yogurt sauce. I have noted below the tomato version since the yogurt one is more favoured by the Armenians and Kurds than by the Turks.

Dough
225 g (½ lb) plain flour
1 egg
5 ml (1 teaspoon) salt
water
Filling
450 g (1 lb) minced lamb or beef
1 onion, skinned and finely chopped
15 ml (1 tablespoon) parsley, chopped
1 egg
5 ml (1 teaspoon) salt
2.5 ml (½ teaspoon) freshly ground
    black pepper

Sauce
1.8 litres (3 pints) chicken or vegetable
    stock or lightly salted water
50 g (2 oz) butter
6 tomatoes, blanched, peeled and
    chopped
3 garlic cloves, skinned and finely
    chopped
5 ml (1 teaspoon) dillweed
5 ml (1 teaspoon) basil
5 ml (1 teaspoon) salt
2.5 ml (½ teaspoon) freshly ground
    black pepper

Sift the flour and salt into a large mixing bowl. Make a well in the centre and add the egg. Mix this in and then, adding a little cold water at a time, knead until you have a smooth dough which comes away from the sides of the bowl and your fingers easily. Continue kneading for a few minutes and then set aside.

In another bowl mix together the minced meat, onion, parsley, egg and seasonings.

Flour a large working surface. Divide the dough into two pieces as this makes it easier to roll out. Roll out the first ball until it is as thin as possible. Cut out as many circles of pastry about 2.5–3.5 cm (1–1½ inches) in diameter as possible. Gather up the scraps, roll out and cut more circles. Repeat with the other ball of dough.

Place a small ball of the meat mixture in the centre of each circle of dough.

Dampen the edges of one circle with cold water and then pinch the edges of the pastry up to make 4 corners which trap the meat inside but do not hide it completely from view. Continue until you have used up all the ingredients.

In a large saucepan bring the stock or water to the boil. Put the *manti* in gently and simmer for 30 minutes.

Melt the butter in a small pan, add the chopped tomatoes and fry for 2–3 minutes. Add the remaining ingredients, mix well and then stir this tomato mixture into the soup and simmer for a further 10 minutes. Taste to check the seasoning and add a little more water if the sauce is too thick.

Serve in individual bowls with bread.

'THE CURSE OF ALLAH BE ON ME.'

*One day a group of the Hodja's friends decided to go on
a picnic. One said, 'The meat for the Şiş Kebab is on me.'
Another added, 'The meat for the Kuzu Kapama is on me.'
A third added, 'I'll supply the Tavuk Kebabi.'
A fourth undertook to pay for all the fruit and
vegetables necessary.
It was the Hodja's turn. He got up, stroked his long, grey
beard and beamed at everyone. 'Friends,' he said, 'we now
seem to have all we need for the picnic. So for my part, may
I add, should this feast last for years and I miss a day
of it, let the curse of Allah be on me!'*

PILIÇ TOPKAPI

Topkapi Palace-Style Poussins

Named after that magnificent palace whose name literally means 'the gate of the cannon'.
It was built in the 15th century and subsequently enlarged. Today Topkapi is a museum
where some of the most precious works of art from all over the world are gathered.

3 poussins *or* 1.5–1.75 kg (3–4 lb)
  chicken
45 ml (3 tablespoons) butter
1 small onion, skinned and finely
  chopped
225 g (8 oz) chicken livers or lamb's
  liver, finely chopped
30 ml (2 tablespoons) raisins

2 large tomatoes, blanched, peeled and
  chopped
5 ml (1 teaspoon) allspice
7.5 ml (1½ teaspoons) salt
1.2 litres (2 pints) water
30 ml (2 tablespoons) pine kernels
175 g (6 oz) long grain rice, washed
  under cold water and drained

If using poussins cut each into 8 pieces – 2 wings, 2 drumsticks, 2 thighs and 2
breasts. If using a chicken cut it into small pieces.

Melt 30 ml (2 tablespoons) of the butter in a large saucepan, add the chicken
pieces and fry for a few minutes, turning once. Add the onion and liver pieces
and fry for a further 3–4 minutes, stirring regularly.

Stir in the raisins, tomatoes, allspice, salt and water and bring to the boil.
Simmer for 10–15 minutes.

Meanwhile melt the remaining butter in a small pan, add the pine kernels and
fry until golden. Stir the contents of this pan into the large saucepan and add the
drained rice. Cover the pan, lower the heat and simmer for 15–20 minutes or
until the chicken and rice are tender.

Transfer to a serving dish, sprinkle with the parsley and serve with a *pilav* or
potatoes and cooked vegetables or a salad.

GÂVÛR DOLMASI
Stuffed Mixed Vegetables

'Destiny,
What a dark fate is mine!
I know nothing about counting,
I am an accountant.
The dish that I like best

Is stuffed egg-plants.
It doesn't agree with me.
I know a freckled girl,
I love her,
She doesn't love me.'

THE STAR AND THE CRESCENT

— • • —

Dolma in Turkish means 'fill' or 'stuff' and this method of cooking usually means that a vegetable is filled with rice or rice and meat and then cooked in a sauce. There are many such dishes in Turkish cuisine, but I hasten to add that this method is not Turkish. It is, in fact, much, much older – as most things in Turkey tend to be.

You can prepare many vegetables, apart from those mentioned in this recipe, in the same way – onions, pumpkin, marrows and many more.

Gâvûr Dolmasi is a selection of vegetables and, as the name *Gâvûr*, meaning Christian, suggests, it is of Armenian origin.

Burghul, cracked wheat, is often used instead of rice and this is popular with the Kurds of Turkey as well as the Armenians.

4 medium aubergines
4 medium courgettes
4 medium green peppers *or* 4 large
    tomatoes
Filling
675 g (1½ lb) minced lamb or beef
1 onion, skinned and finely chopped
225 g (8 oz) long grain rice, washed
    thoroughly under cold water and
    drained
30 ml (2 tablespoons) chopped parsley
1 garlic clove, skinned and crushed
30 ml (2 tablespoons) tomato purée

5 ml (1 teaspoon) salt
2.5 ml (½ teaspoon) freshly ground
    black pepper
2.5 ml (½ teaspoon) chilli pepper
Sauce
60 ml (4 tablespoons) tomato purée
3 litres (5 pints) water
10 ml (2 teaspoons) salt
5 ml (1 teaspoon) chilli pepper
7.5 ml (1½ teaspoons) dried mint
4 garlic cloves, skinned and halved
juice of 1 lemon

Cut the stalk ends off the aubergines and courgettes. With an apple corer remove as much of the flesh as possible from the vegetables leaving a shell about ½ cm (¼ inch) thick. Take care not to split or puncture the shells.

Slice 3 mm (⅛ inch) off the tops of the tomatoes or green peppers and remove the seeds and pith.

Prepare the filling by placing all the ingredients in a large bowl and kneading until well blended.

Fill each vegetable with the stuffing until three-quarters full. This leaves room for the rice to expand while cooking.

Arrange the vegetables in a large, deep saucepan with their open sides uppermost. If there is not room for them in a single layer, place the aubergines and courgettes at the bottom and the tomatoes or green peppers on top.

Cover the vegetables with a plate and place a small weight on top. This prevents the vegetables from moving about while cooking.

Mix all the sauce ingredients together in a large bowl and pour into the saucepan. Bring to the boil, lower the heat and simmer for about 1 hour or until the *dolmas* are cooked. Test with a fork; if the prongs slide in and out easily then they are cooked. Add a little more water during the cooking if necessary. The vegetables must always be completely covered.

Serve hot with a fresh salad of your choice and some yogurt.

KARNI YARIK

Anatolian Baked Stuffed Aubergines

— • ● • —

These are aubergines filled with meat and spices and baked in the oven.

The Greeks have a similar dish called *Papoutsakia* (little shoes). They add 45 ml (3 tablespoons) of grated cheese to the filling. Serve with a rice *pilav*, pickles and salad.

6 medium aubergines
120 ml (8 tablespoons) oil
30 ml (2 tablespoons) butter
1 large onion, skinned and finely
  chopped
550 g (1¼ lb) minced lamb or beef
4 tomatoes, blanched, peeled and
  chopped
45 ml (3 tablespoons) parsley, chopped

7.5 ml (1½ teaspoons) salt
3.25 ml (¾ teaspoon) freshly ground
  black pepper
2 garlic cloves, skinned and crushed
200 ml (7 fl oz) stock or water, boiling
2.5 ml (½ teaspoon) salt
7.5 ml (1½ teaspoons) dillweed
30–45 ml (2–3 tablespoons) lemon juice

Cut the stems and hulls off the aubergines and discard. Peel each aubergine lengthways in 1-cm (½-inch) strips to create an attractive stripy appearance.

Heat the oil in a large frying pan, add the aubergines, 2 or 3 at a time, and fry gently, turning frequently, until they are soft on all sides. Remove with a slotted spoon and drain on kitchen paper. Arrange the aubergines side by side in a shallow ovenproof dish.

Melt the butter in the frying pan with any remaining oil, add the onion and fry until soft. Add the meat and fry, stirring frequently to break up any lumps, until lightly browned. Add half the chopped tomatoes and cook for a further 5 minutes, stirring frequently. Stir in the parsley, salt, black pepper and garlic and cook for a further 10 minutes. Remove from the heat.

One at a time slit the aubergines lengthways to within 2 cm (¾ inch) of either end and only down into the middle of each vegetable. Gently ease each slit open a little to form a pocket.

Fill each pocket with some of the minced meat and place the remaining chopped tomato over the top.

Add the boiling stock or water, sprinkle with the salt and dillweed and cover. Bake in an oven preheated to 350°F (180°C) gas mark 4 for 30 minutes. Uncover, add the lemon juice, re-cover and bake for a further 10–15 minutes. Serve hot.

IZMIR KÖFTESI
Meatballs in Tomato Sauce
———— •●• ————

This is one of my childhood favourites. Once upon a time an aunt of mine married a man from Greece who was in love with this dish. He had it for breakfast, lunch and supper – or so I was told. Well, every time we visited our aunt we were inevitably served this dish of spicy meatballs in a tomato sauce accompanied by plain spaghetti. This was all very well, but my aunt was a terrible cook and did no justice to this fine dish – which brings me to the moral of my story. It does not matter how often you practise a tune on the fiddle it will never sound right unless you have a love for it.

4 slices white bread, crusts removed
675 g (1½ lb) lean lamb or beef, minced twice
1 egg, beaten
2 garlic cloves, skinned and crushed
2.5 ml (½ teaspoon) cinnamon
5 ml (1 teaspoon) paprika
7.5 ml (1½ teaspoons) salt
3.25 ml (¾ teaspoon) freshly ground black pepper

45–60 ml (3–4 tablespoons) flour
45 ml (3 tablespoons) butter
6 large tomatoes, blanched, peeled, seeded and chopped
2 green peppers, chopped
600 ml (1 pint) water
5 ml (1 teaspoon) salt

Soak the bread in a little water and then squeeze dry and crumble into a large bowl. Add the meat, egg, garlic, cinnamon, paprika, salt and pepper and knead thoroughly until smooth.

Keeping your hands damp take walnut-sized lumps of meat and roll into balls. Sprinkle the flour over a large plate and roll the balls in it.

Melt the butter in a large saucepan. Add the meatballs, a few at a time, and fry until evenly browned. Transfer to a plate with a slotted spoon and keep warm.

Place the remaining ingredients in the saucepan, bring to the boil and simmer for 15 minutes.

Return the meatballs to the pan and simmer for a further 15–20 minutes. Transfer to a serving dish and serve with a rice *pilav* or spaghetti and a salad of your choice.

TAVUK KEŞKEKI
Festive Chicken and Wheat
———— •●• ————

Keşkek is better known as *harissa* throughout the Middle East, North Africa and parts of the Balkans. It is one of the oldest dishes in the world, dating well back beyond biblical times.

In essence *keşkek* is a porridge of wheat and meat (chicken or lamb). The wheat should be wholewheat, but pearl barley or large grain burghul can be used. If using whole wheat soak it overnight.

In Anatolia *keşkek* is a festive dish, no doubt derived from the pre-Christian and pre-Muslim eras. When the wheat is being harvested and then cooked, all the villagers come out to celebrate with drums, pipes and songs.

If you wish you can substitute the chicken with the same weight of neck of lamb or, as they prefer in Anatolia, neck of sheep.

1–1.5 kg (2–3 lb) chicken, jointed
7.5 ml (1½ teaspoons) salt
50 g (2 oz) butter
2 large onions, skinned and finely
   chopped

5 ml (1 teaspoon) chilli pepper
350 g (12 oz) wholewheat, soaked
   overnight. You can use pearl barley or
   large burghul

Half fill a large pan with water, add the chicken pieces and 5 ml (1 teaspoon) of the salt and bring to the boil. Lower the heat and simmer until the flesh is tender.

Remove the chicken and reserve the stock.

When the chicken is cool enough to handle remove the flesh and discard the bones. Shred the meat as finely as possible and return to the stock.

Melt the butter in a frying pan, add the onion and fry gently for 5 minutes until soft, stirring frequently. Stir in the chilli pepper and remaining salt and add this mixture to the stock. Bring the stock back to the boil.

Drain the wheat and add to the stock. If using pearl barley or burghul then rinse it thoroughly and add to the pan. Lower the heat and simmer for about 30 minutes or until the grains are tender. While it is cooking beat and stir the mixture constantly with a wooden spoon until it has the consistency of smooth porridge. Taste and adjust seasoning if necessary.

Spoon the *keşkek* into individual soup bowls and serve with bread and pickles.

CIZBIZ KÖFTESI

Meat Rissoles

——— · ● · ———

A very popular peasant meal with a wonderful name full of suggestions. *Cizbiz* implies the sizzling, fizzing sounds of a kebab being cooked.

This is really a meat kebab with a slight difference. Bread, traditionally stale bread, as the peasants could not afford to throw anything away, is added to the meat to make a more substantial and economincal meal.

It is eaten with *pilav* or bread and garlic-yogurt is often poured over the top.

675 g (1½ lb) minced lamb *or* beef
1 large onion, skinned and finely
   chopped
1 egg
45 ml (3 tablespoons) parsley, finely
   chopped
7.5 ml (1½ teaspoons) salt

2.5 ml (½ teaspoon) freshly ground
   black pepper
7.5 ml (1½ teaspoons) cumin
juice of 1 large lemon
75 ml (5 tablespoons) water
4 thick slices bread, crusts removed
oil

Place the meat, onion, egg, parsley, salt, pepper and cumin in a large bowl.

Put the lemon juice and water into a bowl and soak the pieces of bread. Crumble the bread into the large bowl and knead all the ingredients together until the mixture is well blended and smooth.

Keeping your hands damp take an egg-sized lump and either roll it out on a clean work top into a sausage shape, or squeeze along a skewer like a kebab.

Brush the meat with oil and cook under a grill or over charcoal for 10–15 minutes or until cooked through, turning frequently.

DIL DOLMABAHCE
Sole with a Tomato and Anchovy Sauce
— • • —

An Istanbul recipe, one that I particularly like, named after the renowned *Baroque cum rococco cum à la oriental* Sultan's Palace in Istanbul. The dish has a lot more purity than its namesake.

6 sole, gutted	1 garlic clove, skinned and crushed
5 ml (1 teaspoon) salt	5 ml (1 teaspoon) grated lemon peel
juice of 1 large lemon	2.5 ml (½ teaspoon) salt
50 g (2 oz) butter	12 anchovies, chopped
about 60 ml (4 tablespoons) flour	5 ml (1 teaspoon) thyme
Sauce	*Garnish*
25 g (1 oz) butter	lemon wedges
1 medium onion, skinned and finely chopped	fresh tarragon leaves
6 tomatoes, blanched, peeled, seeded and chopped	

First prepare the sauce by melting the butter in a pan. Add the onion and fry for 3–4 minutes or until soft. Stir in the tomatoes, garlic, lemon peel and salt and simmer for 2–3 minutes, stirring occasionally. Stir in the anchovies and thyme and simmer very gently for 5–10 minutes or until any liquid in the pan has evaporated. Remove from the heat and keep warm.

Cut the heads off the fish with a slanting cut and then remove the skin of each fish by grasping a raised edge and ripping it off in one or two firm movements. Cut off the lateral fins and then wash the fish and pat dry with kitchen paper.

Rub the salt and lemon juice into the fish.

Melt the butter in a large frying pan. Taking one fish at a time, dip it into the flour until well coated, shake off any excess flour and then place in the pan. Fry for about 8–10 minutes, turning once, until golden and cooked through. Remove with a slotted spoon, place on a large serving plate and keep warm while you fry the remaining fish in the same way.

Place some of the tomato-anchovy sauce on each fish and serve with the garnishes.

RAKI SOSLU LEVREK
Bass in **Raki**

'There are as good fish in the sea as ever came out of it.'
– It doesn't matter, there's plenty more where that came from.
— • • —

Bass is found in abundance in the Mediterranean Sea and is very popular with Turks and Greeks. It is a fine, tasty fish that has a firm flesh, is free from bone and is often cooked whole since it holds its shape well when cooked. This is a relatively new recipe from Istanbul and you will find it served in the expensive – dare I say 'pretentious' – restaurants.

Raki is a Middle Eastern drink known as *ouzo* in Greek and *arak* in Arabic. It is a blending of grape juice and anis.

50 g (2 oz) butter
1 medium onion, skinned and finely
  chopped
6 bass steaks
120 ml (4 fl oz) dry white wine
7.5 ml (1½ teaspoons) aniseed
5 ml (1 teaspoon) salt

240 ml (8 fl oz) fish stock or water
60 ml (4 tablespoons) double cream
45 ml (3 tablespoons) *raki*
Garnish
15 ml (1 tablespoon) chopped parsley
15 ml (1 tablespoon) chopped tarragon

Melt the butter in a large saucepan, add the onion and fry for a few minutes until soft. Add the bass steaks and fry for 3–4 minutes, turning once. Add the wine, aniseed, salt and stock and bring to the boil. Cover the pan, lower the heat and cook for 10–15 minutes or until the fish is cooked through.

Lift out the fish steaks, arrange on a serving dish and keep warm.

Return the pan to the heat and boil the pan juices for a few minutes to reduce slightly. Remove from the heat and stir in the cream and *raki*. Pour this sauce over the fish, sprinkle with the garnishes and serve.

ŞARAPLI SAZAN BALIGI

Carp in Red Wine

· ● ·

To eat this Istanbul speciality means to have good taste!

6 carp steaks
150 ml (5 fl oz) vinegar
1 large onion, skinned and finely
  chopped
150 ml (¼ pint) fish stock *or* water
50 g (2 oz) sultanas
50 g (2 oz) walnuts *or* hazelnuts, finely
  chopped
30 ml (2 tablespoons) lemon juice

150 ml (¼ pint) dry red wine
5 ml (1 teaspoon) salt
2.5 ml (½ teaspoon) freshly ground
  black pepper
Garnish
30 ml (2 tablespoons) parsley, finely
  chopped
lemon slices

Place the fish steaks in a large, shallow dish and sprinkle with a little salt. Cover with the vinegar and onion and set aside for 2 hours.

Transfer the pieces of fish to a large saucepan, cover with the stock or water and simmer until the fish is tender.

Remove the pieces of fish with a slotted spoon, arrange on a serving plate and keep warm.

Add the remaining ingredients to the stock, stir well and simmer until the sauce is reduced a little. Pour over the fish, sprinkle with the garnishes and serve with a rice *pilav* or potatoes.

LEVREK FILETOSU BEYLERBEYI
Bass Beylerbey Style
— • • • —

Beylerbey is a small, picturesque village near Istanbul where once the sultans and their entourages spent their time relaxing, drinking and, needless to say, wenching.

Mushrooms, tomatoes and onions are fried and served with bass steaks to make a very tasty meal. Serve with a fresh salad and/or a rice *pilav*. Other fish can be prepared in the same way.

6 bass steaks
2.5 ml (½ teaspoon) salt
juice of 1 lemon
30–45 ml (2–3 tablespoons) flour
50 g (2 oz) butter
Vegetables
60–75 ml (4–5 tablespoons) oil
1 bunch spring onions, thinly sliced
  including green heads
1 garlic clove, skinned and crushed

100 g (4 oz) mushrooms, wiped clean
  and thinly sliced
4 large tomatoes, blanched, peeled and
  chopped
5 ml (1 teaspoon) salt
5 ml (1 teaspoon) paprika
Garnish
30 ml (2 tablespoons) parsley or
  coriander, finely chopped
lemon wedges

Arrange the steaks on a large plate, sprinkle with the salt and lemon juice and set aside for 2 hours, turning once or twice during that time.

Meanwhile prepare the vegetables by heating the oil in a frying pan. Add the spring onions and garlic and fry for 2–3 minutes until soft. Add the mushrooms and fry for 2 minutes, stirring frequently. Now add the tomatoes, salt and paprika, stir well and simmer for 5–10 minutes, stirring from time to time. Set aside.

Melt the butter in a large frying pan. Dip the fish steaks into the flour, shake off any excess and place in the pan. Fry for 10–15 minutes, turning once, until golden and cooked through. Meanwhile heat the vegetable mixture.

When the fish is cooked arrange on a large dish, cover with the hot vegetables, garnish and serve.

KÂĞITTA BARBUNYA
Red Mullet in Foil

'Every fish that escapes appears great'
— • • • —

This is one of the most popular fish in the Middle East, beloved of the Greeks, Lebanese and the Turks. The seafronts of Izmir, Istanbul and all the other coastal towns are filled with restaurants where the most prized dishes are fried and grilled red mullet. Usually the larger ones are grilled and the smaller ones fried.

The recipe below however is another popular one, where the fish are cooked in foil. Traditionally cooking parchment was used but it has, in most places, been supplanted by foil. The flesh of this particular fish is full of flavour and this method of cooking retains all that delicate flavour and aroma. Other fish such as trout are also delicious when cooked in this way.

6 medium red mullet, leave the heads
  and tails on and clean out thoroughly
60 ml (4 tablespoons) olive oil
juice of 2 lemons
60 ml (4 tablespoons) parsley, finely
  chopped

5 ml (1 teaspoon) salt
2.5 ml (½ teaspoon) freshly ground
  black pepper
2.5 ml (½ teaspoon) paprika
5 ml (1 teaspoon) thyme

Heat the oven to 190°C (375°F) gas mark 5.

Wash the fish under cold water and pat dry. Rub the fish all over with the olive oil. Place each fish on a piece of foil and wrap each one up so that it is completely enclosed.

Lay them side by side on a baking tray and cook in the oven for 30–45 minutes.

Meanwhile in a small bowl mix the remaining ingredients together.

When the fish are cooked remove from the oven, unwrap and transfer to a serving dish. Sprinkle with the parsley mixture and serve.

SEBZELI BALIK
Fish with Vegetables

Many kinds of fish can be used to prepare this recipe. The traditionally popular ones are bass, cod, hake, whiting and halibut. The vegetables can vary too. You can use mushrooms, tomatoes, green peppers etc. Serve with a rice *pilav*.

60 ml (4 tablespoons) oil
3 large carrots, peeled and sliced into
  1-cm (½-inch) rings
2 sticks celery, sliced into 1-cm (½-inch)
  pieces
3 large potatoes, peeled and cut into
  2-cm (¾-inch) cubes
3 cloves garlic, skinned and finely
  chopped
2 bay leaves

7.5 ml (1½ teaspoons) salt
2.5 ml (½ teaspoon) dillweed
2.5 ml (½ teaspoon) freshly ground
  black pepper
150 ml (¼ pint) water
6 fish steaks
Garnish
30 ml (2 tablespoons) parsley, finely
  chopped
lemon wedges

Heat the oil in a large saucepan or casserole. Add all the ingredients except the water and mix well. Sauté for several minutes, stirring frequently.

Add the water and bring to the boil. Lower the heat and simmer for 10 minutes.

Arrange the fish steaks over the vegetables, cover the pan and continue to cook over a low heat until the fish is tender.

Transfer the fish steaks to a serving dish, spoon the vegetables round them, garnish and serve.

CHAPTER SEVEN

EKMEKLER
Breads

'Bread from a stranger, water from the lake.'
– To live without worries or work.

Bread may be the staff of life, but according to Mahmut Makal, in his village *'apart from the trouble of earning the wretched stuff; it's difficult even to make bread here in any edible form . . . The burden of making this bread, you know, shortens the life of our women by half.'*

BIZIM KOY

There is plenty of bread in Turkey, and Turks are great bread eaters. Indeed 'to dine', in the vernacular, means 'to eat bread'. However, although quantity is there, quality is not. Many tourists and travellers have written about the poor quality of the bread baked in Turkey.

'In some villages,' Makal continues more in sorrow than in anger, *'from autumn on, for weeks on end, it's a never-ending struggle till springtime, baking the bread which is to be eaten, and stacking it up in a corner. Just the bare amount needed is moistened and eaten at each meal.'*

In Eastern Turkey, the Caucasus and Iran this method of bread preservation, preparing huge quantities of it to see them through the harsh winter months until early spring, has been the system for thousands of years, though Makal's village bread is not the same as the famed *lavash*, but an ordinary, thickish loaf which naturally goes stale and hardens. *Lavash* is the classic bread of the Armenians and it is much baked in Turkey where the local name is *Kavgîr*. *Kavgîr* is a large, thin bread usually made with white flour, although wholemeal is sometimes used. It is usually about 60 cm (2 feet) in diameter. At each baking enough is prepared to last for 3–4 months. It is wrapped in linen until required. It is usually prepared in a *tandir* (oven), but sometimes also on a large, circular, dome-shaped piece of cast iron called a *saj* which is heated from underneath by burning cow dung, wood chippings or logs.

'As a matter of course, every house had its own oven (tandir) *where the daily bread was baked – to have to use another's oven was shame and disgrace for any self-respecting housewife ... the oven was a deep pit sunk in the floor, with the fire at the bottom of it, so that the sides – on which the dough was stuck for baking in big flaps – ...'*

THE ASSYRIANS

This then is a *tandir* in which not only breads, but also kebabs and stews (*firin kebabs*) were, and are still, being baked.

KEBAP PIDESI
Bread for Kebab
· ● ·

This is a poor man's version of the great Syrian bread *Khubz Shami* – Damascus bread, better known outside the Middle East as pita bread.

The whole concept behind pita bread is that when it is heated it bloats to form a cavity where fillings of meat and salads are put. Unfortunately this Turkish *kebap pidesi* rarely opens and the bread is wrapped around the meat and then consumed. This recipe then is offered out of interest. I suggest that when you are cooking kebabs you buy the commercially baked pita bread, round or oval, in which to put your meat.

15 g (½ oz) fresh yeast *or* 7 g (¼ oz) dried yeast	450 g (1 lb) plain flour
10 ml (2 teaspoons) salt	*Glaze*
300 ml (½ pint) warm water	milk

Place the yeast, salt and water in a bowl and stir vigorously for 3 minutes.

Sift the flour into a large bowl and make a well in the centre. Gradually work in the yeast mixture with a wooden spoon. Transfer to a floured surface and knead for about 10 minutes or until you have a smooth dough. Place in a clean bowl, cover with a tea towel and leave in a warm place for 30 minutes.

Return to the floured surface and knead for 2–3 more minutes. Divide the dough into 6 apple-sized portions. Roll them between your palms to form smooth balls.

Flour the work top and then flatten each ball with the palm of your hand until 0.5 cm (¼ inch) thick. They can be either round or oval. Dust the tops with flour, cover with a cloth and leave for a further 30 minutes.

Preheat the oven to 230°C (450°F) gas mark 8, putting in 2 large, oiled baking sheets halfway through the heating period. When the oven has reached the required temperature brush the bread tops with milk. Slide 1 or 2 onto each hot baking sheet and bake for 5–6 minutes. Slide on to wire racks and cook the remaining ones in the same way.

KIYMA VEYA PEYNIRLI PIDE

Bread Topped with Meat and Cheese

———— •●• ————

A mixture of cheese and minced meat are spread over *kebap pidesi*. This makes a tasty, savoury snack when served with a bowl of salad.

Dough
use the recipe for *Kebap Pidesi*

Meat Mixture
30 ml (2 tablespoons) butter
2 onions, skinned and finely chopped
225 g (8 oz) lean minced meat
5 ml (1 teaspoon) salt
2.5 ml (½ teaspoon) freshly ground
  black pepper
45 ml (3 tablespoons) parsley, finely
  chopped

15 ml (1 tablespoon) chopped fresh mint
  or 5 ml (1 teaspoon) dried mint

Cheese Mixture
175 g (6 oz) grated cheese, feta, haloumi
  or cheddar
2 egg yolks
30 ml (2 tablespoons) fresh dill *or* 15 ml
  (1 tablespoon) dried dillweed

Topping
1 large egg mixed with 30–45 ml
  (2–3 tablespoons) milk

First prepare the meat mixture by melting the butter in a small saucepan. Add the onions and fry for several minutes until soft. Add the meat and fry for 10–15 minutes, stirring frequently to break up any lumps and to prevent sticking. Stir in the remaining ingredients and remove from the heat.

Now prepare the cheese mixture by placing the cheese, egg yolks and dill in a small saucepan and cooking for 2–3 minutes, stirring constantly. Remove from the heat.

Prepare the dough according to the instructions for *Kebap Pidesi*. While the 6 loaves are resting for 30 minutes mix the meat and cheese toppings together.

When the loaves are ready place 1–2 tablespoons of the filling on each one. Using your fingers spread the mixture out to within 1 cm (½ inch) of the edge of the dough. Using the tips of your fingers, press them into the dough all around the edge of each loaf to make a pattern.

Now very carefully, using both hands, lift one loaf up, hold it about 60 cm (2 feet) above the work top and let it drop down. This will enlarge it. Repeat with the remaining loaves.

Arrange on greased baking sheets, leaving a little space between them, cover with a cloth and leave for a further 10–15 minutes. Heat the oven to 230°C (450°F) gas mark 8.

Brush the top of each with the egg-milk mixture and bake in the oven for 10–12 minutes. The dough should be lightly golden, but still soft enough to fold. Serve hot.

KAVGÎR
Village Bread
· • ·

15 g (½ oz) fresh yeast *or* 7 g (¼ oz) dried yeast	675 g (1½ lb) plain flour
5 ml (1 teaspoon) sugar	5 ml (1 teaspoon) salt
lukewarm water	40 g (1½ oz) yellow cornmeal
	40 g (1½ oz) plain flour

Place the yeast in a small bowl with the sugar and dissolve in 300 ml (½ pint) warm water. Set aside for about 10 minutes in a warm place or until the mixture begins to froth.

Sift the 675 g (1½ lb) flour and salt into a large bowl. Make a well in the centre and slowly work in the yeast mixture and enough warm water to make a stiff dough. Knead on a floured surface for about 10 minutes until the dough is smooth and elastic. Place the ball of dough in a clean bowl, cover with a cloth and leave in a warm place for about 2–3 hours or until it has doubled in size.

Transfer the dough to a floured surface, punch it down and knead again for a few minutes. Return to the bowl, cover and leave for a further 30 minutes.

Flour the work surface again. Divide the dough into apple-sized balls. This amount of dough should make about 12–15 balls.

Mix the cornmeal and remaining flour together in a bowl. Roll each ball of dough in this mixture until well coated.

With a long rolling pin roll out each ball into a thin sheet about 20–25 cm (8–10 inches) in diameter. Sprinkle the work top with flour to prevent sticking.

Line the bottom of the oven with foil and heat the oven to 200°C (400°F) gas mark 6. Place 1 sheet of dough on the foil and cook for about 3 minutes. Remove the cooked *kavgîr* and cover with a tea towel while you cook the remaining *kavgîr* in the same way. Serve immediately.

If they are not used at once then, when completely cold, fold and wrap them in a tea towel and then in plastic or wrap and freeze. When ready to serve them, sprinkle them lightly with water, wrap in a tea towel and leave for 10 minutes to absorb the moisture and to soften.

Variation
ACMA EKMEGI
Doughnut-Shaped Village Bread
· • ·

These very simple, very primitive breads are popular in Central Anatolia. They are round, with a hole in the middle and are sometimes glazed with egg yolk. To prepare, follow the recipe for *Kavgîr,* but omit the yellow cornmeal and flour coating. Instead of rolling each ball into a thin sheet, sprinkle a work top and your hands with flour, roll each one into a sausage-shape about 20 cm (8 inches) long. Join the ends and pinch tightly to secure. Brush the surface of each with egg yolk and then bake in an oven preheated to 190°C (375°F) gas mark 5 for 15–20 minutes or until risen and light golden.

PIDE
Festive Bread
———— • • • ————

'*The bread was in the form of large, round, flattish pancakes, about an inch thick and well browned on the outside; not quite unleavened, for the dough had risen in the baking, but with a texture and flavour utterly different from ordinary bread. I asked if it had a special name, but our host, apparently surprised at the question, replied that it hadn't; "Ekmek-tir", he replied simply; "It's bread."* '

EAST OF TREBIZOND

This bread, perhaps the only genuinely Turkish one, is called *pide* and is not to be confused with the better known variety, *pita* bread which is now available throughout Britain.

Pide is the bread prepared for the Bayram (Muslim Ramazan). It is usually 30–37.5 cm (12–15 inches) in diameter and about 5 cm (2 inches) thick. Sometimes it is topped with nuts and fennel seeds as well as the usual sesame seeds. It can, of course, be much larger as is shown below in a description written by Evliya Effendi in 1637 when the Guilds of Professions in the jurisdiction of the four Mollas of Constantinople paraded in front of the Emperor.

'*They (the breadmakers guild) also make for this occasion immense loaves, the size of the cupola of a haman (public bath), covered with sesamum and fennel; ... no oven being capable of holding loaves of so large a size, they bake them in pits made for that purpose, where the loaf is covered from above with cinders, and from the four sides baked slowly by fire ... Besides these they bake some small sorts of bread and cake called Ramazan Pideh, sumum and lawasha, which they throw out in the Emperor's presence.*'

NARRATIVE OF TRAVELS

Here then is a simplified version of *Pide*.

25 g (1 oz) fresh yeast *or* 15 g (½ oz) dried yeast	15 ml (1 level tablespoon) salt
5 ml (1 teaspoon) sugar	45 ml (3 tablespoons) sugar
60 ml (2 fl oz) warm water	1 egg, beaten
50 g (2 oz) butter or margarine	*Topping*
180 ml (6 fl oz) milk	milk
180 ml (6 fl oz) water	25 g (1 oz) sesame seeds
675 g (1½ lb) plain flour	7.5 ml (1½ teaspoons) fennel seeds

Place the yeast, sugar and 60 ml (2 fl oz) warm water in a small bowl, mix well and set aside in a warm place for 10 minutes or until the mixture has begun to froth.

Put the butter, milk and water in a small saucepan and warm gently until the fat has melted.

Sift the flour and salt into a large bowl and mix in the sugar. Make a well in the centre and add the yeast mixture and butter mixture and stir in with a wooden spoon until you have a soft dough. Transfer to a floured surface and knead for about 10 minutes or until the dough is smooth and elastic.

Grease a large circular dish about 30 cm (12 inches) in diameter. Place the dough in the centre and gently press it down to form an even circle of dough, leaving about 2.5 cm (1 inch) empty all around the edge of the dish. Cover with a tea towel and leave to rise in a warm place for about 1½ hours.

Heat the oven to 190°C (375°F) gas mark 5.

Brush the loaf with milk and sprinkle the sesame and fennel seeds evenly over the surface. Take a sharp knife and make patterned incisions e.g. criss-crosses, over the top.

Bake in the oven for about 40 minutes or until well risen and golden brown. Remove from the tin and cool on a wire rack.

Throughout the major Turkish cities *francala*, white 'Beyaz' or wholemeal is the standard fare. It is really an ordinary English loaf, though larger. In the cities also French sticks, finger rolls, buns, *tost ekmegi* – sliced bread etc are popular. Only in the countryside do *kavgîr*, *acma ekmegi* or *cavdar ekmegi* appear. As for *pide*, it really only comes on the scene during the 40 days of the Muslim festival of Ramazan (Bayram).

CAVDAR EKMEGI
Rye Bread
———— • • • ————

After wheat, rye is the most important European cereal and its original homeland was modern Turkey and the Caucasus. In parts of Anatolia bread is prepared from rye flour or a mixture of rye and plain flour.

These are round, brown-coloured breads with a pleasant flavour, but one of their most important characteristics is that they keep fresh for a long time and in Anatolia this is an inestimable quality.

25 g (1 oz) fresh yeast *or* 15 g (½ oz) dried yeast	450 ml (¾ pint) tepid water
5 ml (1 teaspoon) sugar	675 g (1½ lb) rye flour
	5 ml (1 teaspoon) salt

Place the yeast in a bowl with the sugar and half the water. Stir and set aside in a warm place for 15–20 minutes.

Sift the flour and salt into a large bowl and make a well in the centre. Add the yeast mixture and stir in with a wooden spoon. Gradually add the remaining water and knead until you have a soft dough. Transfer to a floured work top and continue to knead for 8–10 minutes or until the dough is smooth and elastic.

Place the ball of dough in a clean bowl, cover with a cloth and leave in a warm place for about 2 hours or until it has doubled in size.

Return the dough to the floured work top, punch down and knead for a further 2–3 minutes. Divide the dough in half and shape each into a ball by repeatedly drawing the sides down and folding them underneath to make a smooth top.

Place each on a greased baking sheet and flatten slightly with your hand to form a round, cob loaf. Cover with cloths and leave in a warm place for 30–40 minutes or until they have doubled in size.

Bake in an oven preheated to 180°C (350°F) gas mark 4 for about 40–45 minutes or until well risen and golden brown. Makes two 450 g (1 lb) loaves.

CHAPTER EIGHT

TURŞULER
VE SALCALAR
Pickles and Sauces

'One vinegar seller is not like another vinegar seller'

When in season vegetables and certain fruits are pickled in great quantities, packed into large earthenware jars, to last a whole year.

The most popular vegetables are carrots, aubergines, courgettes, cucumbers, artichokes, onions, okra, cauliflower and small, sweet peppers. The latter are substituted by small, green, hot chillies in the southern part of the country. All varieties of pickles appear on a dinner table and the average Turkish housewife never – well hardly ever – buys commercially prepared pickles.

The first recipe is for a cucumber pickle. The cucumbers are 7.5–10 cm (3–4 inches) long and have a sweet taste. They were famed even in the heyday of the Roman gourmet Apicius who makes several references to the cucumbers of Cappadocia and Cilicia.

Small pickling cucumbers can be purchased from Indian grocers. They are not quite the same as the renowned Turkish Adana cucumbers, but they will do.

HIYAR TURŞUSU
Pickled Cucumbers

—— • • • ——

1.2 kg (2½ lb) small, pickling cucumbers	240 ml (8 fl oz) white or cider vinegar
750 ml (1¼ pints) water	4 large garlic cloves, skinned and halved
50 g (2 oz) coarse salt	8 sprigs fresh dill

Scrub and rinse the cucumbers thoroughly. Prick each one 3 or 4 times with a fork.

Bring the water to the boil in a saucepan. Add the salt and vinegar and stir until the salt has dissolved.

Wash and dry two 1.2 litre (2 pint) wide-neck jars. Place 2 half cloves of garlic and 2 sprigs of dill in the bottom of each jar. Pack the cucumbers in tightly and place the remaining garlic and dill on top. Pour the hot brine over the cucumbers to cover and place a small, flat, clean stone over the cucumbers to keep them submerged. Loosely cover the jars and set them aside in a warm place for 3–4 days, then cover tightly and refrigerate.

BIBER TURŞUSU
Green Pepper Pickles

—— • • • ——

For this recipe you need small green chilli peppers which are found in all Indian green-grocers, and many supermarkets. Do not seed them since the best part of the pickle is its 'hot' flavour, that is, of course, if you like hot food!

900 g (2 lb) green chilli peppers	10 ml (2 teaspoons) salt
900 ml (1½ pints) white wine vinegar	60 ml (4 tablespoons) sugar

Wash the peppers and then pack into 2 large, sterilised pickling jars.

Sprinkle 5 ml (1 teaspoon) salt and 30 ml (2 tablespoons) sugar into each jar and then pour in the vinegar. Make sure all the peppers are covered and top up with more vinegar if necessary.

Seal the jars tightly and leave for at least 3–4 weeks.

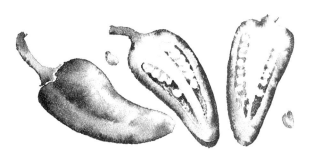

PATLICAN TURŞUSU
Aubergine Pickles
——— • ● • ———

900 g (2 lb) aubergines
1 stick celery, cut into 2.5 cm (1-inch) pieces
225 g (½ lb) carrots, peeled and cut into quarters lengthways and then into 2.5 cm (1-inch) pieces
3–4 red chillies, quartered and seeded

4–5 garlic cloves, skinned
5 sprigs parsley, broken into smaller pieces
900 ml (1½ pints) white wine vinegar
60 ml (4 tablespoons) salt
5 ml (1 teaspoon) mustard seeds

Parboil the aubergines in a large saucepan and then drain. When cool enough to handle squeeze out as much water as possible.

Cut the aubergines into quarters. If they are large cut into smaller pieces of about 5 cm (2 inches).

Now pack all the vegetables into 1 or 2 large sterilised pickling jars.

Place the vinegar, salt and mustard seeds in a saucepan and heat until the salt has dissolved. Pour over the vegetables until they are completely covered. Top up with more vinegar if necessary. Seal tightly and leave to stand for at least 3–4 weeks.

SALCALAR
Sauces
——— • ● • ———

The Turkish cuisine is not very rich in sauces. It has absorbed a large number of French-inspired sauces which, although much used, are not included in this book. Those that are included are more representative of the cuisine, although a few still are of foreign origin like *terbiye*, which, in fact is the Greek *avogolemono*; *samersakli yogurt*, which is the Armenian *sukhdoradz madzoon* and *tarator* which is the Lebanese *taratour*.

SAMERSAKLI YOGURT
Garlic Yogurt Sauce
——— • ● • ———

This is an extremely versatile sauce. It is usually spooned over fried vegetables such as aubergines and courgettes and it generally accompanies *dolmas*. It is also served with minced meat kebabs and with many vegetable dishes.

1 garlic clove, skinned
2.5 ml (½ teaspoon) salt

300 ml (½ pint) yogurt
2.5 ml (½ teaspoon) dried mint

In a small bowl crush the garlic and salt together until pulpy. Stir in the yogurt, cover and chill for 2–3 hours.

When serving, sprinkle the mint over the surface.

DOMATES SALCASI

Tomato Sauce

——— • • • ———

This is a versatile sauce which is used over *pilav* dishes, with roasts and especially with kebabs.

45 ml (3 tablespoons) butter
1 onion, skinned and finely chopped
675 g (1½ lb) tomatoes, blanched, peeled and chopped
1 garlic clove, skinned and crushed
30 ml (2 tablespoons) parsley, finely chopped

2 bay leaves
5 ml (1 teaspoon) salt
1.25 ml (¼ teaspoon) freshly ground black pepper
2.5 ml (½ teaspoon) allspice

Melt the butter in a saucepan, add the onion and fry for several minutes until soft. Stir in all the remaining ingredients, cover the pan and cook over a low heat for about 15 minutes. Stir occasionally to prevent sticking.

Serve hot.

SALATA SALCASI

Lemon Sauce

——— • • • ———

Also known as 'Turkish salad dressing', this is a very popular sauce throughout the Middle East.

Traditionally it is served with fish as well as with salads and cold vegetable dishes.

90 ml (6 tablespoons) olive oil
90 ml (6 tablespoons) lemon juice
2.5 ml (½ teaspoon) salt
1.25 ml (¼ teaspoon) freshly ground black pepper

60 ml (4 tablespoons) finely chopped parsley

Place the oil, lemon juice, salt and pepper in a bowl and mix well. Stir in the parsley, transfer to a sauceboat and serve.

YAYLA SALATA SOSU

Village Salad Sauce

——— • • • ———

A delicious sauce which is ideal with all salads and with cold, cooked vegetable dishes.

150 ml (¼ pint) olive oil
60 ml (4 tablespoons) yogurt
juice of 1 lemon
5 ml (1 teaspoon) salt

2.5 ml (½ teaspoon) icing sugar
1.25 ml (¼ teaspoon) freshly ground black pepper

Mix all the ingredients well in a bowl or pour into a jar and shake well before serving.

TARATOR
Garlic and Walnut Sauce

*'The number of walnuts he has cracked
passes the thousands.'*
– His stupidities are past counting.

————— •●• —————

A wonderful sauce to serve with fish and poultry dishes.

100 g (4 oz) walnuts
3 garlic cloves, skinned
2.5 ml (½ teaspoon) salt

2 slices bread, crusts removed
30 ml (2 tablespoons) lemon juice
olive oil

Pound the walnuts with the garlic and salt in a mortar or grind in an electric blender.

Soak the bread in a little water and then squeeze out.

Spoon the nut mixture into a bowl, add the bread and mix thoroughly. Little by little add the lemon juice and enough oil for the sauce to become thick and smooth.

Serve in small dishes beside each plate.

TARATOR ÇAMFISTIKLI
Pine Kernel Sauce

————— •●• —————

Excellent with all cold meats as well as salads.

100 g (4 oz) pine kernels
2 garlic cloves, skinned
5 ml (1 teaspoon) salt

olive oil
lemon juice

Crush the pine kernels either in a mortar or in a blender.

In a small bowl crush the garlic with the salt until pulpy. Add the ground nuts and mix thoroughly. Little by little add enough oil to make a thick sauce. Now thin this a little with lemon juice. Taste as you go along and adjust the seasoning if necessary.

TERBIYE
Lemon and Egg Sauce

'Let onions grow in his navel.'
– A curse.

————— •●• —————

This is undoubtedly the most popular sauce in Turkey. Of Byzantine origin, it is used in soups, salads, vegetables and with fish dishes.

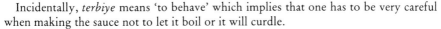
Incidentally, *terbiye* means 'to behave' which implies that one has to be very careful when making the sauce not to let it boil or it will curdle.

2 eggs
juice of 1 lemon
240 ml (8 fl oz) chicken or meat stock

1.25 ml (¼ teaspoon) salt
1.25 ml (¼ teaspoon) freshly ground
   black pepper

Beat the eggs in a bowl with a whisk until frothy. Add the lemon juice, a few drops at a time, and continue whisking.

Thoroughly stir in the stock and seasoning. Transfer to a small pan and cook over a very low heat, stirring constantly, until the sauce thickens. Do not allow the sauce to boil or it will curdle.

TARATOR SADE

Garlic Sauce

'If one does not eat garlic – one does not smell.'

———— · ● · ————

Use with cold meats and also fish and salads.

2 cloves garlic, peeled
5 ml (1 teaspoon) salt

60 ml (4 tablespoons) olive oil
30 ml (2 tablespoons) lemon juice

In a small bowl crush the garlic with the salt. Add 30 ml (2 tablespoons) of the oil, stir well and set aside for 10 minutes.

Stir in the remaining oil and the lemon juice and spoon over meat or vegetables.

TATLILAR
Desserts

'Manage with bread and butter until Allah brings the sweetmeats'

In the old days it was only at ceremonies such as weddings, circumcisions, anniversaries and so on, that desserts appeared. The remainder of the year people waiting impatiently for a wedding or festival lived on fruits, fresh or dried. It is not surprising therefore that many Turkish desserts have religious or festive connotations. Equally, it is not surprising that the mass of the people eat fresh fruit and fruit compotes for desserts and that, although initially surprising, very few people indeed regularly indulge in such desserts as *baklava* or *kadayif*. Outside the major cities and main provincial towns these pastries only appear on the home table on special occasions.

It was in the Seraglio and the houses of the rich that the celebrated Middle Eastern pastries were developed. From the simple Armenian recipe for *baki-halva* (*paklava* or *baklava*), which was prepared on Easter Sunday, many variations were concocted by the chefs in the Sultan's kitchens.

In the countryside people made their own simpler, but not necessarily less delicious, desserts such as *aşure*, often making use of whatever ingredients were available locally.

Today there are many dessert shops selling the pastries and cakes for which the Ottoman cuisine was justly famed. I have selected below a few of the more popular ones.

BAKLAVA
Flaky Pastry with Nuts
————— · • · —————

This is of a Christian festive (Lent) origin. The symbolism behind it was that each layer of pastry, 40 in all, represented the 40 days of Lent when people abstained from meat, fish and eggs. On Easter Sunday, after church, people gathered at home and broke their fast. The highlight of this day was a large tray of home-made *baki-halva* – literally meaning 'Lent sweet'. There are many such pastries in Turkish cuisine. Apart from the standard filling, I have included a few others which you can try for a change.

450 g (1 lb) packet *filo* pastry (see
  Glossary)
225 g (½ lb) unsalted butter, melted and
  with froth removed
225 g (½ lb) walnuts, chopped or
  coarsely ground

Syrup
350 g (12 oz) sugar
15 ml (1 tablespoon) lemon juice
30 ml (2 tablespoons) rosewater

First prepare the syrup. Place the sugar, lemon juice and 350 ml (12 fl oz) water in a saucepan and bring to the boil. Lower the heat and simmer for about 10 minutes or until the syrup leaves a slightly sticky film on a spoon. Add the rosewater and set aside to cool. Heat the oven to 180°C (350°F) gas mark 4.

Most packets of *filo* pastry have sheets about 53 × 28 cm (21 × 11 inches), but it is not easy to find a tin of these dimensions. I use one 30 × 20 cm (12 × 8 inches) and trim the sheets to make them fit. I slip the trimmings between the sheets, maintaining an even thickness. The tin should be at least 2.5 cm (1 inch) deep. Grease this tin with a little melted butter.

Open out the sheets of pastry and cover with a tea towel. Lay 2 sheets of the pastry on top of each other in the tin, keeping those not in use covered so that they do not dry out. Dribble a tablespoon of the melted butter over the second sheet. Repeat in this way until you have 6–8 sheets in the tin. While layering these sheets try to press on them as little as possible. This ensures that air is trapped between the layers and so enables the sweet to rise.

Spread half the nuts over the top sheet of pastry. Continue with layers of pastry and spoonfuls of butter until you have laid down a further 6–8 sheets. Spread the remaining nuts evenly over the last sheet laid down.

Continue layering the pastry with spoonfuls of the melted butter dribbled over alternate sheets until you have used up all the pastry. Lightly brush any remaining butter all over the last sheet so that every bit of pastry is covered. Again take care not to press down on the pastry.

Cut the *baklava* into lozenge shapes, using a sharp knife and taking care to press as little as possible on the pastry. Place in the oven and cook for 30 minutes. Lower the temperature to 150°C (300°F) gas mark 2 and bake for a further hour or until the pastry is golden.

Remove the *baklava* and set aside to cool a little. Then pour the cold syrup all along the gaps in the warm *baklava*. Set aside until completely cold.

To serve, first run a sharp knife along the gaps to make sure that all the layers have been completely separated. Lift the pieces out and arrange on a serving dish.

Variations You can substitute the walnut filling with almonds, pistachios or coconut. You can also use fruit fillings such as oranges, apples, cherries, pineapples and even pumpkin.

KABAK BAKLAVASI
Pumpkin Baklava
———— • ● • ————

450 g (1 lb) *filo* pastry (see Glossary)
225 g (½ lb) unsalted butter, melted and
   with froth removed
Syrup
see above

Filling
225 g (½ lb) pumpkin, peeled and grated
225 g (½ lb) caster sugar
100 g (4 oz) walnuts, chopped or
   coarsely ground
15 ml (1 tablespoon) rosewater

Mix all the filling ingredients together in a bowl.

Prepare this sweet as described above, making one layer with the filling rather than two.

KAYMAKLI BAKLAVA
Baklava filled with Cream
———— • ● • ————

This is a classic of the Ottoman cuisine and is popular throughout the Arab world where it is known as *Baklawah Osmanli*.

Although claimed to be made with cream, neither *kaymak* (see Glossary) nor any other kind of cream is used. In fact, the filling is a simple semolina and milk custard.

This sweet has a heavenly taste!

450 g (1 lb) *filo* pastry (see Glossary)
225 g (½ lb) unsalted butter, melted and
   with froth removed
Syrup
225 g (½ lb) sugar
150 ml (¼ pint) water

15 ml (1 tablespoon) lemon juice
Filling
600 ml (1 pint) milk
25 g (1 oz) fine semolina
2.5 ml (½ teaspoon) cinnamon
5 ml (1 teaspoon) rosewater

First prepare the syrup by placing the sugar, water and lemon juice in a saucepan and bringing to the boil. Simmer for 10 minutes and then set aside to cool.

Now prepare the filling by bringing the milk to the boil in a saucepan. Add the semolina, cinnamon and rosewater and simmer very gently, stirring constantly, until the mixture thickens. Set aside to cool.

Heat the oven to 130°C (250°F) gas mark ½.

Open out the *filo* and cover with a cloth. Grease a baking tin about 30×20 cm (12×8 inches) and at least 5 cm (2 inches) deep. Lay 2 sheets of pastry in the tray and then dribble a tablespoon of the melted butter over the second sheet. (Because the size of *filo* sheets varies you may have to trim the edges or fold them over. Any trimmings can be arranged between the sheets to give a uniform thickness.) Repeat this until you have 6 layers of pastry in the tin. Do not press any of the sheets down as you make this sweet.

Pour the filling into the dish and gently spread it out with the back of a spoon to form an even layer.

Now lay a sheet of pastry over the filling and dribble with a little butter. Continue layering the pastry and butter as before until the pastry is finished. Spoon any remaining butter over the last sheet, discarding any milky residue in the bottom of the pan, and lightly brush it out to cover the whole surface.

Place on the top shelf of the oven and bake for 2 hours. Leave the oven door slightly ajar, this will ensure that the pastry stays white.

Remove from the oven and set aside for 20 minutes. Cut with a sharp knife into 5 cm (2 inch) squares. Pour the syrup along the gaps in the *baklava* and leave to cool completely before serving.

THE WAYS OF THE LORD

One hot summer's day Hodja Nasurettin was relaxing in the shade of an almond tree. As he sat there happy and contented he could not help but compare the large pumpkins growing on vines with the small almonds growing on a tall majestic tree.

'Sometimes I just cannot comprehend the ways of Allah!' he thought. 'Just fancy permitting such tiny almonds to grow on so majestic a tree and huge, monstrous pumpkins on such delicate vines!'

Just then an almond snapped off and fell smack on to his bald head. He got up at once and, lifting his hand to heaven he cried, 'Oh Allah in Heaven, forgive my doubting mind. You are all-wise, all-knowing, for where would I have been now if pumpkins grew on trees!'

KÖROĞLU SARMASI
Cheese and Coconut Pastries

— • ● • —

These pastries are usually prepared with a special dough which, although similar to *filo* pastry, is slightly thicker. I have suggested below that you prepare these sweets with a double thickness of *filo* pastry.

The traditional cheese is *Bolu* – a well-known goat cheese of Turkey. This is almost impossible to obtain in this country and so I suggest you try feta, or a similar white crumbly cheese.

450 g (1 lb) *filo* pastry (see Glossary)
225 g (½ lb) unsalted butter, melted and
  with froth removed
Filling
450 g (1 lb) white cheese. If using feta
  cheese soak it in cold water for 12
  hours, changing the water several
  times. This helps to get rid of the salt.

225 g (½ lb) desiccated coconut
Syrup
450 g (1 lb) sugar
600 ml (1 pint) water
juice of 1 lemon

Drain the cheese and cut into ½-cm (¼-inch) chunks. Place in a bowl, add the coconut and mix well.

Heat the oven to 180°C (350°F) gas mark 4.

Lay the *filo* out flat on a work top and cover with a cloth to prevent it drying. Take one sheet of pastry, lay it out flat and brush its surface with melted butter. Lay another sheet of *filo* over the buttered one.

Take a long, thin rolling pin about 1 cm (½ inch) in diameter (or a long stick or even a thick knitting needle) and position it 2.5 cm (1 inch) in from one of the shorter sides. Sprinkle a little of the filling, as evenly as possible, all along the inner edge of the rolling pin. Carefully fold the pastry over the pin and then fold the pin over the filling. Fold over once more and then brush a narrow strip of pastry along the edge of the pin with butter. Fold over once more and cut along the edge with a knife. Do not fold more than 4 times.

Carefully push the rolled pastry from both ends inwards to make the roll shorter and to create wrinkles and folds. Take care or the filling will burst through the pastry. Very carefully pull out the stick. Transfer this pastry to a buttered baking sheet and place with the joint underneath.

Continue in this way until you have used up all the ingredients. I was able to make 3 pastries from each 2 sheets of *filo*, but whether or not you will be able to do so will depend on the size of the sheets.

Arrange all the pastries on buttered baking trays, packing them quite tightly together. Use any remaining butter to brush the tops of all the pastries. Bake in the oven for about 30 minutes or until golden.

Meanwhile prepare the syrup by placing the sugar, water and lemon juice in a saucepan and bringing to the boil. Simmer for 10–15 minutes and then set aside.

Remove the pastries from the oven and leave for 10 minutes. Then cut each pastry in half and pour the warm syrup over them. Set aside to cool and then serve.

Tel-Kadayif
Shredded Pastry with Nuts

· ● ·

This pastry is prepared in a similar method to *baklava*; only the dough is different. You can use any of the fillings suggested for *baklava*. *Tel-kadayif* is the Arab *kunafeh*, which was so highly prized in the days of the Califs of Baghdad, and about which poets sang their praises. The Turks, via their imperial conquests, took many dishes from the Arabs and one such is the recipe below which they, in confusion, call *tel-kadayif* (from the Arab *atayef* meaning pancake).

450 g (1 lb) *kadayif* pastry (see Glossary)
350 g (12 oz) unsalted butter, melted and
  with froth removed
Filling
175 g (6 oz) walnuts, chopped or
  coarsely ground
30 ml (2 tablespoons) sugar

10 ml (2 teaspoons) cinnamon
Syrup
350 g (12 oz) sugar
juice of 1 lemon
350 ml (12 fl oz) water
30 ml (2 tablespoons) rosewater

First prepare the syrup by placing the sugar, lemon juice and water in a saucepan. Bring to the boil, lower the heat and simmer for about 10 minutes or until the syrup forms a slightly sticky film on a spoon. Remove from the heat, stir in the rosewater and set aside.

Heat the oven to 180°C (350°F) gas mark 4.

Lightly brush a baking tin, about 30×22.5 cm (12×9 inches) or about 25 cm (10 inches) in diameter and at least 2.5 cm (1 inch) deep, with a little of the melted butter.

Put the pastry into a large bowl and gently ease apart the strands without breaking them. Remove any hard nodules of pastry which you may find in some brands.

Pour three-quarters of the melted butter into the bowl and gently rub all the strands between your fingers until they are well coated with the butter.

Divide the pastry into 2 equal parts and spread one part evenly over the base of the tin. Mix the filling ingredients together and spread evenly over the pastry. Press the filling down firmly. Arrange the remaining pastry evenly over the top, tuck in any strands hanging over the sides and press the pastry down firmly.

Spoon the remaining melted butter evenly over the top, discarding the white residue in the bottom of the pan. Place in the oven and cook for 30 minutes. Lower the heat to 150°C (300°F) gas mark 2 and cook for a further 1½ hours or until golden.

Remove from the oven and pour the syrup slowly over the *kadayif*, covering as much of the surface as possible. Cover the sweet with kitchen foil, place a large board over the top and add a heavy weight in order to compress the *kadayif*. Leave until cold and then cut into squares or lozenges about 3.5–5 cm (1½–2 inches) in size.

Variations substitute the walnuts with 175 g (6 oz) of either coarsely chopped pistachios or almonds.

YOĞURT TATLISI
Yogurt Sweet
———— • • • ————

One of the most popular cakes throughout the Middle East, this is a sponge made from *labna* (concentrated yogurt), soaked in syrup. It and similar sweets are of ancient origin, probably Assyrian.

Labna is very popular among Syrians, Kurds and Armenians. It makes an excellent breakfast when topped with a little olive oil and a few black olives, and eaten with thin oriental bread.

For *Yoğurt Tatlisi*, you first have to make the *labna*: Pour 300 ml (½ pint) natural yogurt into a large muslin bag or tea towel lining a colander. Gather up the top and tie tightly with string. Suspend it over the sink or a bowl and leave to drain overnight. The thick cream left in the bag is *labna*.

100 g (4 oz) *labna* – you can prepare this
  amount from about 300 ml (½ pint)
  yogurt
100 g (4 oz) sugar
5 ml (1 teaspoon) bicarbonate of soda
3 eggs, beaten

175 g (6 oz) plain flour, sifted
Syrup
350 g (¾ lb) sugar
450 ml (¾ pint) water
15 ml (1 tablespoon) lemon juice

First prepare the syrup by placing all the ingredients in a saucepan and bringing to the boil. Simmer for 10 minutes and then set aside to cool.

Place the labna in a large bowl, add the sugar and bicarbonate of soda and stir for 2–3 minutes. Add the eggs and beat thoroughly. Add the flour, little by little, and mix thoroughly.

Heat the oven to 200°C (400°F) gas mark 6.

Grease and liberally flour a baking tin about 17.5×27.5 cm (7×11 inches). Pour in the *labna* mixture and smooth over the surface with the back of a spoon. Bake in the oven for 20–25 minutes.

Remove from the oven, cut into 5-cm (2-inch) squares and pour the cool syrup evenly over the top. Set aside to cool.

KIZ-MEMESI TEL-KADAYIF
'Young Girls' Breasts'
———— • • • ————

As the name implies these pastries are meant to be small, rounded and firm and each is topped with a walnut! The filling suggested below is chopped almonds, but you can substitute hazelnuts, pistachio nuts or a mixture of coconut and chopped walnuts.

450 g (1 lb) *kadayif* pastry (see Glossary)
225 g (½ lb) unsalted butter, melted and
  with froth removed
about 12 walnut halves
75 g (3 oz) almonds, finely chopped

Syrup
700 g (1½ lb) sugar
450 ml (¾ pint) water
15 ml (1 tablespoon) lemon juice

Open out the shredded pastry on a work top and discard any coarse bits. Now

shred the pastry very finely with your hands or pass it through a mincer. The aim is to get very small, fine pastry strands. Drop the pastry into a large bowl and then pour most of the melted butter over the top. Mix and rub with your hands until all the pastry shreds are coated with the butter.

Heat the oven to 180°C (350°F) gas mark 4.

Lightly brush 2 baking trays with a little of the remaining butter.

To make these sweets in the correct shape you need a soup ladle about 6 cm (2½ inches) in diameter, or a container of a similar shape and size. Lightly brush the inside of the ladle with a little melted butter. Put one of the walnut halves in the bottom of the ladle. Fill the ladle with shredded and buttered pastry and press down. Make a hole with your index finger in the centre of the pastry, large enough to take 10 ml (2 teaspoons) of the chopped nuts. Push the nuts in.

Add a little more pastry to cover the nuts and press down as hard as possible to make a firm mould. Place your fingers over the mouth of the ladle, turn it over and then lift the ladle off. Transfer the pastry to the baking tray.

Continue making pastries in this way until you have used up all the ingredients. Place the baking trays in the oven and bake for 40 minutes.

While they are cooking prepare the syrup. Place the sugar, water and lemon juice in a saucepan and bring to the boil. Simmer for about 10 minutes.

When the pastries are cooked, remove from the oven. Bring the syrup back to the boil and then ladle the syrup over the pastries. Set aside to cool and then serve them by themselves or with cream.

Here is a little story of blackmail. The village teacher (Hodja), in lieu of payment, would accept food, particularly *baklava*, but the poor people could not even afford fat.

'But there's no fat in the house,' a mother said. 'One can't send just any food to the Hodja. He'll certainly want at the very least some noodles, some manti, *and some* baklava; *and one wants a lot of fat for* baklava.' *So she loaded her husband up with a bushel of rye that she had in the house and sent him off to market. 'We must have some fat for the Hodja's meal,' she declared. 'But my dear, the Hodja is an ordinary person like us; can't he eat what we do?' 'Ah,' she said, 'the Hodja warned the children; God eats* baklava *every day; if the Hodja doesn't eat it, too, God won't be pleased. He'll think less of us and be angry.'*

BIZIM KOY

PEYNIR TATLISI
Cheese Fingers in Syrup

• • •

A Turkish speciality of white cheese mixed with butter, eggs and flour and then soaked in syrup. These fingers are really magnificent when served cold with a little of their own syrup and some whipped or clotted cream. In Turkey they are served with *kaymak* – Turkish clotted cream (see Glossary).

The flavour of the fingers is often varied by adding *a*) the grated rind of 2 lemons, *b*) 45 ml (3 tablespoons) of ground pistachio nuts or *c*) 60 ml (4 tablespoons) of desiccated coconut.

Syrup
900 g (2 lb) sugar
1.2 litres (2 pints) water
juice of 1 lemon
Dough
275 g (10 oz) white crumbly cheese,
  preferably feta, soaked in tepid water
  for 2 hours

100 g (4 oz) unsalted butter
50 g (2 oz) caster sugar
10 ml (2 teaspoons) bicarbonate of soda
3 eggs
225 g (8 oz) plain flour
75 g (3 oz) cornflour

First prepare the syrup by placing the sugar, water and lemon juice in a saucepan and bringing to the boil. Lower the heat and simmer for 10–15 minutes or until it forms a thin film on a spoon. Set aside.

Heat the oven to 160°C (325°F) gas mark 3.

Drain the soaked cheese and squeeze in a muslin bag or between kitchen paper to remove any liquid. The cheese must be dry and should now weigh about 225 g (8 oz).

Place the butter, sugar and bicarbonate of soda in a large bowl and beat until smooth and creamy. Crumble the cheese and add to the mixture. Add the eggs and stir until the mixture is well blended. Sift in the flour and cornflour. First mix in with a wooden spoon and then knead with your hands until the mixture is smooth and forms a ball. It may be necessary to add a sprinkling of flour if the mixture is a little sticky.

Grease 2 large baking trays. Using a 2 cm (¾ inch) nozzle, pipe fingers about 6 cm (2½ inches) long on to the baking trays, placing them 2.5–3.5 cm (1–1½ inches) apart.

Place in the oven and bake for 15 minutes. Remove the trays from the oven, brush each cheese finger with hot water and then cover with a cloth for 3–4 minutes. Bring the syrup back to the boil.

Remove the cloth and pour ¾ of the boiling syrup evenly over the fingers and return to the oven. Cook for about 30 minutes or until the fingers are golden brown. While they are cooking turn them 2 or 3 times so that they absorb as much syrup as possible. Remove from the oven and leave to cool.

Serve cold with the remaining syrup and some cream.

RAHAT LOKUM
Turkish Delight
—— • • ——

If there is anything truly 'Turkish' in the repertoire of so-called Turkish delicacies and desserts it is *Rahat Lokum* which, literally translated, means 'a morsel of rest'. These are the delicacies with which, for centuries, the ladies of the harems passed their monotonous lives fattening themselves for the greater pleasures of their lords and masters. For the Ottomans, like the Arabs, liked big, buxom women and there was a tradition, which for all I know might still exist in the provinces, whereby women were bought and sold by their weight – the bigger the more expensive!

The accepted masters of this delicacy is a family-run business, which has been in existence for well over 200 years, called Hadji Bekir. In my opinion their produce is the best in the world.

The recipe below will in no way do justice to this magnificent sweet, but not only will you have the satisfaction of making you own, but it will also still taste much better than any commercial brand.

Rahat Lokum comes in many different versions, ranging from plain or with nuts to those filled with soft fruit, or covered in chocolate or coconut. The recipe below is for Turkish delight with nuts, but if you prefer it plain then simply omit the nuts. You could also try omitting the nuts and adding a few tablespoons of strained jam instead to make *Meyveli Lokum* – fruit-filled Turkish delight.

5 ml (1 teaspoon) butter
450 g (1 lb) sugar
300 ml (½ pint) water
5 ml (1 teaspoon) lemon juice
25 g (1 oz) gelatine dissolved in 120 ml (4 fl oz) hot water
2.5 ml (½ teaspoon) vanilla essence
15 ml (1 tablespoon) rosewater

3 drops natural food colouring, red, green or gold
15 ml (1 tablespoon) pistachio nuts, halved
50 g (2 oz) icing sugar
25 g (1 oz) cornflour

MAKES ABOUT 30 PIECES

Grease a 15-cm (6-inch) square baking tin with the butter and set aside.

Put the sugar, water and lemon juice in a saucepan and bring to the boil. Continue boiling until the temperature reaches 130°C (250°F) on a sugar thermometer. If you do not have one then drop a little of the syrup into a bowl of cold water. If it has reached the required temperature it will form a hard ball.

Remove the pan from the heat and leave to stand for 10 minutes.

Stir in the dissolved gelatine and the vanilla essence and beat with a wooden spoon until well blended. Pour half the mixture into the baking tray.

Stir the rosewater and colouring into the remaining mixture and mix well.

Meanwhile sprinkle the halved nuts over the mixture in the tin. Pour the remaining mixture into the tin and set aside in a cool place overnight.

Sift the icing sugar and cornflour on to a large plate.

Turn the *lokum* out on to a clean board and cut into 2.5-cm (1-inch) cubes. Toss the cubes in the sugar mixture and make sure they are thoroughly coated. Shake off any excess sugar.

Either wrap each piece in waxed paper or store in an airtight container.

EKMEK TATLISI
Bread Pudding
·•·

The thrifty Anatolian housewives never wasted anything. They even created a 'school' of desserts based on stale bread. Well, perhaps this is a slight exaggeration! There is a special dough for this kind of sweet and I have given it below. However, you can use ordinary, stale or otherwise, white or wholemeal sliced bread.

The choice of fruit topping can vary. The most popular ones are black cherries, apples, quinces or strawberries.

Kalip Ekmegi – **dough**
15 g (½ oz) fresh yeast
200 ml (7 fl oz) milk
450 g (1 lb) plain flour

5 ml (1 teaspoon) salt
50 g (2 oz) icing sugar
50 g (2 oz) unsalted butter
3 egg yolks

Dissolve the yeast in a cup with a few tablespoons of the milk, warmed, and set aside for about 10 minutes or until the mixture begins to froth.

Sift the flour, salt and icing sugar into a large bowl. Add the butter and rub in until it resembles fine breadcrumbs. Make a well in the centre and add the yeast mixture and egg yolks and mix with a wooden spoon. Add the milk, little by little and, after thoroughly mixing, knead for 10–15 minutes until the dough is smooth and elastic. Cover with a cloth and leave in a warm place for 30 minutes.

Heat the oven to 130°C (250°F) gas mark ½.

Lightly sprinkle a work top with flour and divide the dough into 2 equal portions. Take one ball and roll out until ½ cm (¼ inch) thick. Cut into rounds with a 7.5-cm (3-inch) pastry cutter. Gather up the scraps, roll out again and cut into more rounds. Repeat with the other ball of dough.

Place the rounds on greased baking sheets and cook in the oven for 30 minutes. Remove and leave for 4–5 hours.

The rounds are ready to be used in a bread pudding. The ones you do not need can be stored in an airtight tin.

VIŞNELI EKMEK TATLISI
Bread Pudding with Cherries
·•·

This is the most popular bread pudding in Turkey. You can use tinned cherries, but if they are sweetened then omit the sugar and water and use the tinned syrup, made up to 300 ml (½ pint) with water if necessary. The recipe can be used for other fruit too, apples, pears or quinces. Prepare as for the cherries below.

Bread
8 portions *kalip ekmegi* (see above) *or*
  8 thin slices stale bread
Topping
75 g (3 oz) unsalted butter

450 g (1 lb) morello cherries, stoned *or*
  any other kind in season *or* tinned
  cherries
225 g (8 oz) icing sugar
250 ml (8 fl oz) water

Heat the oven to 180°C (350°F) gas mark 4.

Spread the slices of bread or pieces of *kalip ekmegi* generously with the butter, trimming off any crusts. Arrange in a large, shallow, ovenproof dish and bake in the oven until lightly golden.

Meanwhile place the fresh cherries, icing sugar and water in a saucepan, mix well and bring to the boil. Boil vigorously for 2 minutes and then lower the heat and simmer for about 10 minutes or until the syrup becomes sticky and coats a spoon. If using tinned cherries drain the syrup into a small pan, make up to 300 ml (½ pint) with water if necessary and simmer for 4–5 minutes.

Remove the bread from the oven, pour the cherries and syrup evenly over it and then return to the oven and bake until most of the syrup has been absorbed.

Remove from the oven and serve hot with *kaymak* or whipped cream.

A PIOUS CUSTOMER

*One day the Hodja, seated in his stall, was selling figs
that had arrived in the morning fresh from Ismir.
A woman came along and asked if she could buy a few
pounds of those delicious figs and pay later. Business being
slack the Hodja accepted and weighed the required amount.
He then picked one and asked the woman to taste for
herself that they were truly magnificent.
'Thank you vey much,' said the woman, 'but I have
to refuse. You see, today I am fasting. Some years ago I
had been ill and couldn't fast during the month of Ramazan.
I am fasting now to make up for the days I
missed then!'
On hearing this the Hodja grabbed the bag of figs
out of the woman's hand and cried aloud, 'I am very sorry
madam, but I have changed my mind about selling
to you on credit.'
'But why, Hodja Effendi?'
'Because madam, if it takes you years before you start
paying God his due heaven alone knows how long
it will take you to pay me!'*

TAVUK GÖĞSÜ
Chicken Breast Pudding

'Not from one's hands, but one's teeth – can one save!'

• ● •

One of the most splendid desserts of the Ottoman Turkish cuisine. The chicken is cooked with milk, sugar and cream and served chilled.

breast of half a chicken
enough water or dry white wine to cover
   the chicken
900 ml (1½ pints) milk
300 ml (½ pint) single cream
1.25 ml (¼ teaspoon) salt

175 g (6 oz) sugar
45 ml (3 tablespoons) ground rice
30 ml (2 tablespoons) cornflour
Garnish
5 ml (1 teaspoon) cinnamon

Place the chicken breast in a saucepan and add enough water or dry white wine to cover by 1 cm (½ inch). Bring to the boil and then lower the heat and simmer until almost tender. Drain the chicken and then finely shred it or pass it through a mincer.

Return the meat to a saucepan, add sufficient water to cover by 1 cm (½ inch) and bring quickly to the boil. Spoon off any fatty residue that comes to the surface. Drain, add fresh water and bring to the boil again. Again remove any fatty residue and then drain and set aside.

Put the milk, cream, salt and sugar in a saucepan and bring slowly to the boil, stirring constantly until the sugar has dissolved.

Place the ground rice and cornflour in a small bowl and mix to a smooth paste with a little cold water. Add this mixture to the simmering milk and continue cooking, stirring constantly, until the mixture thickens. Stir in the chicken and cook over a very low heat for a few minutes, stirring frequently to prevent the mixture sticking to the pan. Set aside to cool a little.

Pour the sweet into individual dishes and chill until ready to serve and then sprinkle with cinnamon.

AŞURE
Vegetable and Rice Pudding

• ● •

This is a traditional rice pudding from Anatolia which incorporates locally grown and seasonably available vegetables and fruits such as haricot beans, chickpeas, figs and apricots. It is often made for large parties such as weddings, when it is freely distributed to friends, neighbours and passersby.

Traditionally this sweet is made with hulled wheat (*bugday*), which can be found in most health food shops, but if it is not available you can use large grain burghul instead. Some people like to purée the rice after it has been cooked and often the water is replaced by milk – in which case the sweet is known as *Beyaz Aşure* – white rice pudding.

50 g (2 oz) haricot beans, soaked overnight in cold water
50 g (2 oz) chickpeas, soaked overnight in cold water
50 g (2 oz) large grain burghul (cracked wheat)
50 g (2 oz) long grain rice
900 ml (1½ pints) water or a mixture of milk and water
150 ml (¼ pint) milk

225 g (8 oz) sugar
50 g (2 oz) sultanas
4 dried figs, chopped
4 dried apricots, chopped
10 ml (2 tablespoons) rosewater
40 g (1½ oz) walnuts, coarsely chopped
25 g (1 oz) pine kernels
25 g (1 oz) pistachio nuts, halved
25 g (1 oz) butter
SERVES 8–10

Place the haricot beans and chickpeas in separate saucepans with their soaking water, bring each to the boil and then simmer until tender. The beans will take about 1 hour and the chickpeas a little longer. Add more boiling water if necessary.

Rinse the burghul and rice thoroughly and place in a saucepan with the water. Bring to the boil, lower the heat and simmer for 20–30 minutes. When tender strain the beans and chickpeas and add to the pan together with the milk and simmer for a further 10 minutes. Add the sugar, sultanas, figs, apricots and rosewater, stir thoroughly and simmer for another 10 minutes. Stir in the nuts and butter. By now the mixture should resemble thick porridge. If you think it is still a little think then simmer for a few more minutes, stirring frequently.

Remove from the heat and leave to cool a little. Pour into individual bowls or a large, decorative serving dish and decorate, forming patterns with some combination of the following: sultanas, cinnamon, pomegranate seeds, chopped blanched almonds or walnut halves.

'WHAT HAS IT GOT TO DO WITH YOU?'

One day the Hodja was approached by a man who was notorious in the village as a gossip, and the Hodja disliked him for it.
'Hodja Effendi,' he said, as if imparting a tremendous secret, 'I just saw the sweet-maker's son carrying a huge tray of beautiful, white baklava.'
'What has that got to do with me?' said the Hodja.
'But Hodja Effendi, I think I noticed it was being taken to your house!'
'Then what has it got to do with you?' was the curt reply.

KAYMAKLI ELMA KOMPOSTOSU
Apples with Cream

— • • —

An interesting characteristic of Turkish desserts in general is the clever and, quite often, bewilderingly simple use of fruits – fresh or dried. While the Persians will offer you a bowl of fresh fruits as a dessert, the Turks will inevitably tempt you with a wide range of *kompostolar*. These are dried or fresh fruits, dropped into water or syrup and then cooked on a low heat until tender. They are served chilled with *kaymak* or fresh cream or often, especially in the villages, with natural yogurt.

All kinds of fruits are used – quinces, apples, pears, apricots, peaches, strawberries, oranges and more.

Dried fruits can also be prepared in this way and often several different fruits are cooked together.

300 ml (½ pint) water	**Garnish**
275 g (10 oz) sugar	180 ml (12 tablespoons) *kaymak* (see
5 ml (1 teaspoon) lemon juice	Glossary) *or* clotted cream *or* whipped
18 cloves	cream
6 large cooking, or firm eating, apples,	45 ml (3 tablespoons) finely chopped
peeled and cored	pistachio nuts or walnuts

Place the water, sugar and lemon juice in a large saucepan and bring to the boil.

Insert 3 cloves around the top of each apple. Place the apples, side by side, in the saucepan and baste with the syrup. Lower the heat, cover the pan and simmer very gently, basting occasionally, until the apples are just tender. The time will vary according to the type of apple, but between 10–15 minutes is normal.

Remove the pan from the heat and set aside to cool. When cold transfer the apples to individual serving dishes, discard the cloves and spoon the cream into the centre of each apple. Pour a little of the remaining syrup over each and sprinkle with the chopped nuts. Chill until ready to serve.

ARMUT KOMPOSTOSU
Pears in Syrup

'Pear, oh pear, come ripen and fall into my mouth.'
– Said of people hoping to obtain something without effort.

— • • —

juice of ½ lemon	600 ml (1 pint) water
900 g (2 lb) firm pears, peeled, quartered	275 g (10 oz) sugar
and cored	3 cloves

Brush the quartered pears all over with the lemon juice. This will prevent them discolouring and give them a glistening sheen.

Place the water in a saucepan, bring to the boil, add the pears and cook for 10 minutes.

Stir in the sugar and cloves, raise the heat and bring to the boil. Immediately lower the heat, stir carefully and cook for a further 15 minutes or until the pears are tender. Remove the pan from the heat and set aside to cool.

Transfer the pears to individual bowls, discarding the cloves, pour a little syrup over them and chill. Serve with cream or yogurt.

IZMIR KOMPOSTOSU

Dried Figs in Syrup

'The fig pips did not even get into my teeth.'
– About trifling or insignificant people
or things.

———— • • • ————

The finest figs in the world grow near the city of Izmir – ancient Smyrna – which was the centre of Hellenic culture and is still today perhaps the most westernised city in the country. There is a certain gentleness and sophistication there which is very lacking in the brash, ultra-modern Ankara and old, tatty, patched-up Istanbul. Izmir was the most cosmopolitan city of the Ottoman Empire where there were more non-Turks and non-Muslims than anywhere else in the Empire.

150 g (5 oz) sugar	**Garnish**
juice of 1 lemon	75 g (3 oz) pistachio nuts or hazelnuts,
600 ml (1 pint) water	finely chopped
450 g (1 lb) dried figs	SERVES 4–6

Place the sugar, lemon juice and water in a saucepan and bring to the boil. Lower the heat and simmer for 5 minutes.

Arrange the figs in the syrup and simmer very gently until the figs begin to 'plump up' and to take on something like their original shape.

Remove the figs with a slotted spoon and arrange in a serving dish. Sprinkle with the nuts and serve warm or cold with tea or coffee.

KAYGANA
Anatolian Sweet Crêpes
————— • • • —————

These are Anatolian-style crêpes that have been popular for centuries. Although there are a few savoury crêpes, the majority seem to be sweet. All kinds of fruit, nut, milk and cream-based *kayganas* are made. Basically they are thin pancakes which are folded over a filling of your choice. In the villages the crêpes tend to be made much thicker than the wafer-thin crêpes of France. Below I have given the basic batter recipe for a thin crêpe.

Batter
225 g (8 oz) plain flour
2.5 ml (½ teaspoon) salt
4 eggs

60 ml (4 tablespoons) melted butter
475 ml (16 fl oz) tepid milk
a little vegetable oil

Sift the flour and salt into a large bowl. Make a well in the centre and add the eggs, one at a time, stirring them in with a wooden spoon. Add the melted butter and stir in thoroughly. Now gradually add the milk, stirring constantly, until you have a smooth batter with no lumps. Cover the bowl with a cloth and leave in a cool place for 1 hour.

With a pastry brush lightly grease a 15–17.5 cm (6–7 inch) heavy-based frying pan with a little of the oil. Place the pan over a moderate heat and warm the oil until it is very hot. Remove the pan from the heat and pour 60 ml (4 tablespoons) of the batter into it. Tilt the pan in all directions to help the batter spread evenly. Return the pan to the heat and cook for 30–40 seconds. Shake the pan gently to loosen the crêpe and then gently lift the crêpe with a palette knife and turn it over. Brown the reverse side for 20–30 seconds and then slide the *kaygana* onto an ovenproof plate and keep warm.

HANIM GOBEGI
'Lady's Navel' Fritters
————— • • • —————

These are delicious fritters which are deep fried then steeped in syrup and filled with whipped cream. The depression in the centre which is filled with cream is meant to represent a lady's navel!

Syrup
450 g (1 lb) sugar
5 ml (1 teaspoon) lemon juice
450 ml (¾ pint) water
Dough
50 g (2 oz) butter
2.5 ml (½ teaspoon) salt

225 g (8 oz) plain flour, sifted
3 eggs
oil for frying
5 ml (1 teaspoon) almond essence
Garnish
150 ml (¼ pint) double cream, whipped

First prepare the syrup. Place the sugar, lemon juice and water in a saucepan and bring to the boil. Simmer for 10 minutes and then set aside to cool.

Place the butter and 300 ml (½ pint) water in a large saucepan and bring to the boil, stirring all the time until the butter melts. Remove from the heat, add the salt and flour and, using a wooden spoon, stir vigorously until the mixture as well blended. Make a well in the centre of the dough and add the eggs, one at a time, and continue to beat until the mixture is smooth, shiny and comes away from the sides of the pan.

Lightly oil your hands and then break off a walnut-sized lump of dough and roll between your palms to form a ball. Place on an oiled baking sheet. Continue until you have used up all the dough. Space well apart on the baking sheet.

Into a large saucepan pour enough oil to cover the bottom by about 5 cm (2 inches) and then heat.

Flatten a few of the balls a little and then, dipping your forefinger in the almond essence, press it about 1 cm (½ inch) into the centre of each one to make a depression. Place a few into the gently sizzling oil and leave to fry for about 8 minutes. Turn once and fry for a further 8 minutes or until the fritters are golden. Do not fry too quickly or the insides will not be cooked. Remove with a slotted spoon and place on kitchen paper to drain, then drop into the syrup, turn once and leave to steep for 5 minutes before transferring, with a slotted spoon, to a serving plate.

Allow the oil to cool a little while you prepare a few more balls and then fry as described above. Continue until all the fritters are fried and steeped in syrup.

Before serving drop 5 ml (1 teaspoon) of the whipped cream into the centre of each fritter.

'REMIND ME TO LOSE MY TEMPER'

One evening Nasurettin quarrelled with his wife and shouted at her so fiercely that she fled for refuge to the neighbouring house, where he followed her. And it so happened that a wedding feast was in progress and all present did all they could to calm old Nasurettin down. They vied with each other to make the couple reconciled to each other. Baklava, kadayif, aşure *and all kinds of* halvas *were offered. The Hodja turned to his wife and said, 'My dear, remind me to lose my temper more often – then life really would be worth living.'*

MEŞRUBATLAR
Drinks

'Pretty wife, old wine – many friends'.

Wat did the nomadic Turkish tribes (Mongolians, Turkomans, Seljuks, Uygurs, Khazaks, Bulgars among others) drink to quench their thirst? They drank water, warm, fresh blood and mare's milk from which they also prepared an intoxicating drink called *koumiss* which is still popular in parts of Russia, Central Asia and the Caucasus, but is almost non-existent in Turkey. What of tea and the famed 'Turkish' coffee?

Tea (*çay*) penetrated the Middle East via Persia (Iran) a few hundred years ago and up until the middle of the 19th century Ottoman Turkey imported all her tea from Iran. Towards the end of that period tea plantations appeared in the region of the Black Sea ports of Trabzon and Rize. The entrepreneurs were, as usual, Armenians or Lazes and the advisers and instructors were English. This sub-tropical region of Turkey was so suitable for tea plantations that today Turkey is self-sufficient and, in fact exports some tea to neighbouring countries.

Tea in Turkey is never drunk with milk. It is made with sugar and is served in little glasses about 7.5 cm (3 inches) high with slightly narrowed necks just below the rims. A great deal of tea is drunk in Turkey. It is offered during all business transactions and there are tea and coffee vendors at every street corner. Tea-boys, carrying brass trays filled with little tea glasses, are to be found zigzagging their way through the multitude of passers-by every minute of the day.

The tea is made in a teapot and left on a kettle which keeps it warm, similar to a Russian samovar, and it is replenished with hot water. Turkish tea is light in colour and taste and has a distinctive, fragrant flavour. It is, unfortunately, rather expensive.

Coffee is Ethiopian by origin, was introduced into Arabia by Arab slave traders and spread throughout the Middle East with the advent of Islam. It acquired its 'Turkishness' via the Ottoman Empire. There is a lovely story that at the siege of Vienna (1529), when the Ottoman armies were finally crushed and retreated in disarray leaving behind all their arms, goods and the conquered loot; the conquerors found scores of sacks filled with pea-shaped grains. From their prisoners they were informed that these black grains were called *kahwah* which the infidels used to boil in water and drink. Thus *Kahwah Turk* first made its appearance in Europe. However, Turkish coffee officially arrived in Istanbul in 1554 and in Europe in 1645, when an Armenian called Haroutyun (Pascal) opened the first coffee shop in Paris.

The Greek god of wine, Dionysus (Bacchus), was born in modern Turkey. Noah planted the first vines when the waters withdrew in Turkey. In short, myth or reality, it was in Asia Minor and the Caucasus that viticulture was first propagated and whence its science (some call it art) spread to the rest of the world.

In the Middle Ages the Califs of Baghdad imported, for their gratification, barrels of wine from Armenia. Equally, the Byzantine emperors satiated themselves with the sweet wines of Crete, Lesbos and the Peloponnese. However, with the advent of Islam the millenniums-old tradition of wine-making, about which several historians, including Herodotus, Xenophon and Strabo, have written in detail, virtually disappeared.

Since 1928 when Islam ceased to be the official religion, the state has promoted the manufacture of liqueurs, wines and beers as well as importing them. However, very little wine is consumed and little is produced. Nevertheless, the quality of that which is bottled is of a high standard.

All drinks in Turkey come under the overall control of the Government State Monopolies. The best vineyards are located in the south of the country and the best known wines, of those exported to Europe, are *Trakya*, a dry white, the full, red *Buzbag* and a lovely wine from European Turkey called *Tekirdag* which is a medium white. All of these are available in Britain.

Some other drinks are Doluca, Kulup, Marmara and Kavaklidere. However, perhaps best-known drink in Turkey is *Raki* (Club, Vatan) which is similar to the Arab *Arak* and the Greek *Ouzo*. And finally, a liqueur of note is *Mersin*, which is made from oranges.

When drinking in Turkey it is always advisable to ask for a bottle of the house wine: *beyaz şarab* – white wine; *kirmizi şarab* – red wine. *Serefe!* (cheers!)

ÇAY KARANFIL
Clove Tea

———— · ● · ————

Tea is very often flavoured with herbs and spices such as aniseed, cinnamon and cloves. For those who suffer with colds, flu and stomach pains the following tea is administered.

900 ml (1½ pints) water   15 ml (1 tablespoon) tea leaves
2 cloves   sugar to taste

Place the water and cloves in a saucepan and bring to the boil. Lower the heat and simmer for 5–7 minutes. Turn off the heat, stir in the tea leaves and sugar to taste and strain into a teapot. Serve.

NB Some people like to add a small cinnamon stick to the water while it is simmering.

In southern Turkey, near the Syrian border, people drink a tea made with aniseed – *Anisonlu Çay* – which is claimed to promote digestion, improve the appetite, relieve flatulence and, in children, colic. So if you suffer from any of these or others then try this excellent intestinal purifier! All you need to do is prepare tea in the usual way and then add 2.5 ml (½ teaspoon) aniseed powder per person and sugar to taste.

KAHVE
Turkish Coffee

'Coffee and tobacco are complete repose.'

———— · ● · ————

The difference between Turkish-type coffee and others is that the former is made from pulverised coffee beans boiled with sugar to produce a thick, syrupy drink.

There are 3 kinds of Turkish coffee:
    sade – without sugar
    orta – medium sweet
    şekerli – very sweet.

When the coffee has been drunk there will be a certain amount of sediment left in the bottom of the cup. For goodness' sake do not try to eat it. I have seen many people try to do this – and just about live to regret it! The only thing one does with the sediment is to get someone else to tell your fortune – along the same lines as reading tea leaves. The predictions are as accurate and interesting as the teller's imagination is vivid. Still, it is a good way to pass time; and in Turkey people have always had plenty of time to pass.

The recipe below is for 1 person. Increase the amounts in proportion to the number of people for whom you are preparing it.

1 coffee cup full of water   5 ml (1 teaspoon) finely ground coffee
sugar to taste

Pour the water into a *jezve* or *ibrik* (the small long-handled brass or copper pot) and add the sugar. Bring to the boil, stirring constantly until the sugar has dissolved. Add the coffee, stir well and bring back to the boil. As the coffee froths up remove the *jezve* from the heat and allow the froth to subside. Return the *jezve* to the heat until the froth rises to the rim again. Remove once again. Repeat this process two more times.

Remove from the heat and pour into a coffee cup. Do not stir or you will disturb the sediment and the coffee will taste gritty.

BOZA
Fermented Millet Drink
· ● ·

This is a bread-based drink particularly popular on the west coast of the country. It is sold on the streets at night and is always accompanied by a handful of roasted chickpeas.

Boza is not really a drink, but more of a light porridge. It is made from stale bread which is cut or crumbled into a large pan, covered with water and left to soak until it ferments and becomes sour. A little milk is added, together with a pinch of cinnamon and it is consumed warm.

AYRAN
Yogurt Drink

'He can't afford a penny for a glass of Ayran,
but will hire a cart to go to the Baths.'
– About people who live beyond their means.

· ● ·

This is the soft drink of the Middle East. It is served throughout the day and is marvellously refreshing in the heat of summer.

In the large cities you will see *Ayrançis*, with their beautifully decorated containers, pouring from a great height (with a lot of showmanship) their ice-cold *ayran* and other drinks to quench the thirst of passers-by. It is a very healthy drink which is easy to make and much, much better than the colas and fizzy drinks of the West.

You can make a large amount and refrigerate it. The proportions given below are for 1 person. Increase the ingredients in proportion to the number of people to be served.

30 ml (2 tablespoons) yogurt 1.25 ml (¼ teaspoon) dried mint
300 ml (½ pint) water ice cubes
1.25 ml (¼ teaspoon) salt

Spoon the yogurt into a glass and slowly stir in the water until the mixture is smooth. Add the salt and mint and mix well. Drop in the ice cubes and serve.

ŞERBETLER
Sherbets

——— • ● • ———

Ayran is not the only soft drink available to a thirsty Turk. He can have a choice of many fresh fruit- and vegetable-based drinks. Street vendors and small corner shops prepare instant fruit juices such as lemon, orange, tangerine, pomegranate, cherry, raspberry, cornelian cherry, strawberry, apple, melon, carrot, tomato, rose petal – all fresh with no preservatives or colourings!

During the days of the sultans, these sherbets were served during all meals – wine and other intoxicating drinks having been prohibited by Koranic law. In Anatolia, after the birth of a child, all the guests are served a glass of cold sherbet – most children here are still born at home.

NAR ŞERBETI
Pomegranate Syrup

——— • ● • ———

'If I had a magic wand
If where I struck
Roses bloomed
Flying roses.

If I had a magic wand
If I could strike a pomegranate tree
And make the pomegranates burst with
laughter.

And baby-faced girls
Stick out their heads
One by one from the boughs.

If I could stuff them into my pockets
And take them to my crystal palace
To live happily ever after
In my fairytale.'

ERCÜMENT BEHZAT LAV – PENGUIN BOOK OF TURKISH VERSE

Pomegranates are squeezed, the juice extracted, mixed with sugar and lemon juice, diluted with water and drunk chilled.

It is a beautiful, light vermilion-coloured, delicious drink.

750 ml (1¼ pints) water	juice of 1 large lemon
450 g (1 lb) sugar	300 ml (½ pint) pomegranate juice

Mix all the ingredients in a saucepan and heat until the sugar has dissolved.

Transfer to a large jug and refrigerate for several hours.

GLOSSARY

BURGHUL
Cracked Wheat
— • • —

Burghul is the staple cereal of many Anatolian villages. It is hulled wheat which is steamed until partly cooked, dried under the sun and then ground into 3 grades:

large – used for *pilavs* and *dolma* fillings   fine – for salads and the famed Syrian-
medium (if available) – for *dolma* fillings   Lebanese *kibbehs*

Burghul is sold in most Indian and Middle Eastern shops and in most health food shops. It is also known as bulghur, bulgar or poogouri.

CLARIFIED BUTTER or GHEE
Süsme Yağ
— • • —

Clarified butter is used extensively in Turkey, particularly when making desserts and pastries. At other times ordinary, salted butter or margarine are used. In the villages, of course, a fat from the tail end of the sheep, *Kuyruk yaği* is still widely used. *Ghee* is available in many supermarkets and in most Indian stores. However, if you wish to prepare your own there is a simple recipe below.

900 g (2 lb) butter

Melt the butter in a saucepan over a low heat. Skim off the foam with a spoon as it appears on the surface. Remove the pan from the heat and leave for 5 minutes.

Skim off any more scum that appears.

Spoon the clear butter into a bowl and discard the white residue left in the bottom of the pan.

Refrigerate the butter until you are ready to use it.

FETA

— • ● • —

A crumbly white cheese usually made from goat's or sheep's milk. As it is preserved in its own salted whey, it may need soaking for 1–2 hours to reduce the saltiness. Feta is now widely available in supermarkets as well as Middle Eastern shops.

FILO PASTRY

— • ● • —

This paper-thin dough is used in the making of pastries such as *baklava*. It can be purchased from Greek, Middle Eastern, some Continental and Indian shops, and in a few supermarkets. It is sometimes sold as *phyllo* pastry or strudel pastry. It freezes successfully. If using commercial pastry follow the instructions below for its use:

Remove the *filo* from its wrapping. Each packet usually weighs 450 g (1 lb) and contains about 20–25 sheets. Sprinkle a little flour over a work top and then gently open the sheets out flat.

Moisten a tea towel until it is evenly damp and spread it over the top of the *filo*.

Remove each sheet as you need it and always remember to cover the remaining ones again.

If cutting the sheets into certain sizes, cover quickly after shaping because *filo* dries out very quickly.

Any sheets not used should be wrapped carefully and returned to the refrigerator or frozen until required.

HALOUMI

— • ● • —

A salty sheep's milk cheese often used for cooking. It is available in Middle Eastern shops.

KAYMAK
Thick Cream

*'You are a gent, I too am a gent – well, who
then is to milk the sheep?'*

———— • ● • ————

Kaymak is the Middle Eastern cream. It is a rich, very thick cream which can literally be
cut with a knife. There is no European equivalent. The nearest I can find is genuine West
Country clotted cream.

Kaymak is usually made from buffalo or sheep milk. The recipe below uses a mixture of
milk and cream and although the result is fairly successful, it is not quite the real thing.

1.8 litres (3 pints) milk   600 ml (1 pint) double cream

Pour the milk and cream into a large, shallow pan. Bring slowly to the boil.
Lower the heat and simmer very gently for 2 hours.

Remove from the heat and leave to rest for 8 hours.

Refrigerate for several hours. By now there should be a thick layer of cream
over the top. Slide a knife around the edge of the pan and carefully lift and
transfer the cream to a serving dish.

Serve with desserts and pastries.

KUNAFEH PASTRY

———— • ● • ————

Dough similar to *filo* pastry, but shredded, used for making *kadayifs*.

PEYNIR
Cheese

———— • ● • ————

There are several fine cheeses in Turkey. Most are made with ewes', sheep and cows' milk.
However goats', as well as mares', milk is also used in parts of Anatolia.

Some of the better known cheeses are:

Beyaz Peyniri – a white cheese made
  fom sheeps' milk
Tulum Peyniri – a large, white, soft
  sheeps' cheese
Lor Peyniri – similar to the Greek feta
  with a soft, crumbly texture.
  Normally made with ewes' or goats'
  milk

Bolu – similar to feta and made from
  goats' milk
Kaser – a dry, hard Cheddar type
Kuflu Peyniri – mouldy, dry, blue,
  Stilton type

These are very difficult to find in this country. For the recipes in this book I
suggest you use feta, haloumi or stated alternatives. Feta and haloumi are both
readily available in many shops and supermarkets. (See above.)

POMEGRANATE SYRUP
Nar Suyu
— • • • —

This is the concentrated juice of the pomegranate and can be bought from some Middle Eastern shops. It is rather expensive and I suggest you try making and bottling your own.

8 large, ripe pomegranates   175 g (6 oz) sugar

Remove the skin of the pomegranates with a sharp knife. Remove the seeds from their hives by tightly squeezing the segments of the fruit in your palms.

Extract the juice either by using a fruit-juicing machine or by placing the seeds, a handful at a time, in a small muslin bag and squeezing the juice into a bowl.

Pour the juice into a saucepan and heat through. Add the sugar and bring slowly to the boil, stirring constantly until the sugar has dissolved. Lower the heat and simmer for 15–20 minutes or until the mixture thickens to a syrup.

Remove from the heat, leave to cool and then store in a glass jar or bottle and use as required.

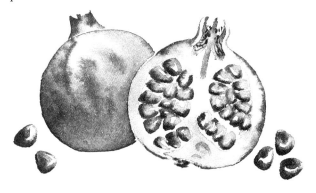

ROASTED NUTS
— • • • —

Almonds, walnuts, pistachios, hazelnuts and pine kernels, as well as chickpeas, sunflower seeds, melon pips and pumpkin seeds are roasted and used in stews, sweets and salads. The simplest way to roast them is to spread the nuts on foil and cook in the centre of a hot oven or under a hot grill until golden, turning them occasionally to prevent burning.

ROSEWATER
Gŭl Suyu
— • • • —

This is distilled from rose petals and is used to flavour puddings and desserts. It can be found in Indian and Middle Eastern stores as well as in many health food and chemist shops.

SUMAK

———— · ● · ————

The dried, crushed berries of a species of the sumach tree. It was used in Roman times and is still very popular in parts of Eastern Turkey, Iran and the Caucasus.

Steep it in water to extract its essence and then use in stews instead of lemon juice.

Do not make your own as some species are poisonous. Always buy it from a reliable Middle Eastern or Greek shop. Ask for Armenian *sumak*.

TAHINA
Sesame Seed Paste

———— · ● · ————

A paste made from toasted and crushed sesame seeds. The finest quality comes from Southern Turkey and Syria.

Tahina is much used in the Middle East in soups, salads and stews. It is the basic ingredient in the popular, commercial *halvas* sold throughout the region. You can purchase bottled or tinned *tahina* in most Middle Eastern and Indian shops and also, now, in many health food shops.

Note that *tahina* separates if it has stood for some time so always stir it before using.

TARHANA

———— · ● · ————

A mixture of burghul and yogurt, dried in the sun, which produces a pasta-like grain, used to add substance to soups and stews. *Tarhana* can be bought from specialist Middle Eastern stores. It is also known as *trahana* (Greek) and *kishk* (Arabic).

TATLI ŞURUBU
Basic Syrup for Sweets

———— · ● · ————

This is a sugar-based syrup that appears throughout the Middle East and is used extensively with pastries.

The sugar is boiled in water to which a little lemon juice is added to prevent crystallisation. Then the syrup is often flavoured with rosewater or orange-blossom water.

450 g (1 lb) sugar
300 ml (½ pint) water
15 ml (1 tablespoon) lemon juice

15–30 ml (1–2 tablespoons) rosewater or
orange-blossom water

Place the sugar, water and lemon juice in a saucepan and bring to the boil. Lower the heat and simmer for 5–10 minutes. The longer the syrup is boiled the thicker it will become, and this is really a matter of choice. In general, the Turks like their syrup lighter than the Arabs and Armenians.

Remove from the heat, add the flavouring of your choice and set aside to cool.

YOGURT

——— · ● · ———

This is one of the most important ingredients in the Turkish cuisine. Yogurt is of Aryan origin, originating in Northern Iran. With the advent of the Aryan races it spread, via Iran, to Asia Minor and later to the Arab lands. Yogurt is eaten as a snack by itself, with sugar, diluted with water to make the well-known *ayran* or *tan*, is mixed with cucumber and mint, or with spinach or is served as a dip. It is also used to make soups, sauces, stews and, sometimes, desserts. It is often served, especially in Turkey, as the final *coup de grâce* to a meal.

Yogurt varies from a smooth, creamy curd which is light in texture and aroma to one which is heavy. It is usually made from sheeps' milk, but camels', buffaloes' and especially goats' milk are also very popular – the latter with Kurdish tribes.

In the small, provincial cities and towns dotted all over Anatolia there are stores that deal exclusively with yogurt where entire families often congregate to taste and then purchase huge quantities of yogurt which is stored in wooden tubs weighing 10–20 kg (22–44 lbs).

One of the most attractive sights in Turkey is that of the yogurt men who call from street to street, hailing the beneficial qualities and high standards of their product. They make their rounds with twin tubs of fresh yogurt swinging from chains suspended from a yoke across their shoulders.

Never keep yogurt too long, even in a refrigerator, otherwise it will turn sour. I am aware that fresh, live yogurt can now be bought in many shops, but I am a traditionalist by nature and have yet to be convinced that any commercial make of yogurt can equal the home-made version.

1.2 litres (2 pints) milk	15 ml (1 tablespoon) 'live' yogurt (called a 'starter')

Bring the milk to the boil in a saucepan. As the froth rises, turn off the heat, then allow to cool to the point where you can dip you finger in and count up to 15, i.e. a temperature of 38°C (100°F).

Put the starter into a cup and stir in 30–45 ml (2–3 tablespoons) of the warm milk. Beat this mixture until smooth, then pour it into the milk. Stir gently and pour into a bowl. Cover the bowl with a large plate and then wrap a towel around the bowl and plate.

Put in a warm place, for example, on top of a cooker or near a radiator; leave for about 8 hours or overnight without disturbing.

Transfer the bowl to the refrigerator.

BIBLIOGRAPHY

All translations in the text are by the author, unless specified.

Yemek Kitabi. Mehmet Yildir Milli Melmud Basimevi. Istanbul 1948

Yemek Öğretimi. Ekrem Muhittin Yegen. Inkilapve Aka. Istanbul 1955

Turk Mutfak Sanati. Necip Usta. Kirel Matbaasi. Istanbul 1976

One Day the Hodja. Murat Hikmet. Tarhan. Ankara 1959

Hodja Nasurettin. ed G. Doniguian. Doniguian Press. Beirut 1976

Bizim Köy. Mahmut Makal Varlik. Istanbul 1950

Köyümden. Mahmut Makal Varlik. Istanbul 1952

Penguin Book of Turkish Verse. ed Nermin Menemencioğlu. Penguin Books 1978

The Star and the Crescent. Illham Berk. trans. D. Patmore. Constable & Co Ltd 1946

The Book of Dreams. Compilation of 17th–19th-century Armenian and Turkish folk beliefs. Aztag Press. Lebanon 1940

The Assyrians and their Neighbours. W. A. Wigram. G. Bell & Son 1929

East of Trebizond. Michael Pereira. Geoffrey Bles 1971

Narrative of Travels. Evliya Effendi. trans. R. J. Von Hammer 1828

The Emergence of Modern Turkey. Bernard Lewis. Oxford University Press 1961

Pre-Ottoman Turkey. Claude Cahen. trans. J. Jones-Williams. Sidgwick & Jackson 1968

Asia Minor. Transcaucasia. ed Major-General Sir Charles Wilson. John Murray 1895

The Harem. N. M. Penzer. Spring Books 1966

Travels in Asia Minor. R. Chandler. British Museum 1971

Turkey Today and Tomorrow. Nuri Eren. Pall Mall Press 1963

The Turks. David Hotham. John Murray 1972

The Development of Secularism in Turkey. Berkes Niyazi. McGill University Press, USA 1964

My Travels in Turkey. D. Cecil Hill. Allen & Unwin 1964

Ottoman Poetry. E. J. W. Gibb. Luzac & Co 1900

INDEX